What People Are Saying About
Stop Resisting Your Sins!

"There is perhaps no better way to serve your own mental health and well-being than by total surrender to love and service on a daily basis. In his book, Eric Roderiques marvelously shows us how this is possible by invoking the intention and visualization of love that is inherent in prayer."
    Dr. Rudolph E. Tanzi,
    Author, *The Healing Self*,
    Professor of Neurology,
    Harvard Medical School

"The book's clear, encouraging language is certain to help.... An intriguing recasting of prayer in the psychotherapy arena."
    - *Kirkus Reviews*

ResistingSins.com

Stop Resisting Your Sins!

Biblical Answers for Transforming Bad Habits, Negative Thoughts, Anger, and Obsessive-Compulsive Disorder

Eric Roderiques

WESTBOW
PRESS®
A DIVISION OF THOMAS NELSON
& ZONDERVAN

Copyright © 2018 Eric Roderiques.

All rights reserved. No part of this book may be used or reproduced by any means, graphic, electronic, or mechanical, including photocopying, recording, taping or by any information storage retrieval system without the written permission of the author except in the case of brief quotations embodied in critical articles and reviews.

This book is a work of non-fiction. Unless otherwise noted, the author and the publisher make no explicit guarantees as to the accuracy of the information contained in this book and in some cases, names of people and places have been altered to protect their privacy.

The information, ideas, and suggestions in this book are not intended as a substitute for professional advice. Before following any suggestions contained in this book, you should consult your personal physician or mental health professional. Neither the author nor the publisher shall be liable or responsible for any loss or damage allegedly arising as a consequence of your use or application of any information or suggestions in this book.

WestBow Press books may be ordered through booksellers or by contacting:

WestBow Press
A Division of Thomas Nelson & Zondervan
1663 Liberty Drive
Bloomington, IN 47403
www.westbowpress.com
1 (866) 928-1240

Because of the dynamic nature of the Internet, any web addresses or links contained in this book may have changed since publication and may no longer be valid. The views expressed in this work are solely those of the author and do not necessarily reflect the views of the publisher, and the publisher hereby disclaims any responsibility for them.

Any people depicted in stock imagery provided by Thinkstock are models, and such images are being used for illustrative purposes only. Certain stock imagery © Thinkstock.

Additional internal art design by Meghan Jackson.

ISBN: 978-1-9736-1445-6 (sc)
ISBN: 978-1-9736-1446-3 (hc)
ISBN: 978-1-9736-1444-9 (e)

Library of Congress Control Number: 2018900492

Print information available on the last page.

WestBow Press rev. date: 01/16/2019

Scripture taken from the NEW AMERICAN STANDARD BIBLE®, Copyright © 1960, 1962, 1963, 1968, 1971, 1972, 1973, 1975, 1977, 1995 by The Lockman Foundation. Used by permission.

THE HOLY BIBLE, NEW INTERNATIONAL VERSION®, NIV® Copyright © 1973, 1978, 1984, 2011 by Biblica, Inc.® Used by permission. All rights reserved worldwide.

Scripture quotations are from the ESV® Bible (The Holy Bible, English Standard Version®), copyright © 2001 by Crossway, a publishing ministry of Good News Publishers. Used by permission. All rights reserved.

The Living Bible copyright © 1971 by Tyndale House Foundation. Used by permission of Tyndale House Publishers Inc., Carol Stream, Illinois 60188. All rights reserved. The Living Bible, TLB, and the The Living Bible logo are registered trademarks of Tyndale House Publishers.

Scripture taken from the Amplified Bible, Copyright © 1954, 1958, 1962, 1964, 1965, 1987 by The Lockman Foundation. Used with permission.

The Holy Bible: International Standard Version. Release 2.0, Build 2015.02.09. Copyright © 1995-2014 by ISV Foundation. ALL RIGHTS RESERVED INTERNATIONALLY. Used by permission of Davidson Press, LLC.

Scripture taken from The Message. Copyright © 1993, 1994, 1995, 1996, 2000, 2001, 2002. Used by permission of NavPress Publishing Group.

Scripture taken from the New King James Version®. Copyright © 1982 by Thomas Nelson. Used by permission. All rights reserved.

For my wife

THE JOSHUA PROTOCOL

- *It's not me.*
- *God, thank you for your forgiveness.*
- *God, thank you for your fellowship.*
- *God, thank you for your discipline.*

*Do not conform to the pattern of this world,
but be transformed by the renewing of your mind.*
Romans 12:2 (NIV)

Acknowledgments

I would like to recognize several people for their encouragement, and for assisting me in writing this book. I wish to thank Jeffery M. Schwartz, M.D., for reviewing and editing the section on Obsessive-Compulsive Disorder. Additionally, I would like to thank William Thomas, M.F.T., for lending me his expertise during the evaluation of my original manuscript. I also would like to thank Daniel E. Jones, Ph.D., a long-time advisor and friend, for offering his fresh and valuable perspectives on this work and for urging me to simply: "Get it done." Thanks also to all my manuscript "field testers." Some of these individuals are actively engaged in the struggle to overcome bad habits. I hope all of them will enjoy greater health, happiness, and success in the future. I appreciate their time, informed input, and encouragement on this project. Furthermore, I would like to thank my wife for her ongoing support for what must seem like an author's quixotic adventure. Lastly, I wish to gratefully acknowledge the gift afforded to me by my brilliant and mysterious mentor, *the Counselor*.

Contents

Introduction xix

Counseling Session 1: Basic Principles 1
Overcoming Human Nature..3
The Human Brain—Made Simple..................................4
An Illustration: You Versus *Not* You..............................8
On The Topic of Evil 10
Meditate on the Bible...11
Celebrate Everything and Transform Bad into Good 13

Counseling Session 2: Building a Relationship with God ..17
The Gibeonite Deception...17
Inappropriate Relationships 18
A Special Prayer 19
Seek Forgiveness...20
Seek Fellowship..22
Seek Discipline 23
Thank Messages 25

Counseling Session 3: Key Concepts Explained 29
Mindfulness 30
The Bodyguard...34
Thoughts on Spiritual Purification..................................36
Healthy Sex: One Love Relationship................................37
Use Discipline to Shape Sexuality..................................39
Scriptures for Defining Godly Discipline 42
Sharing in God's Reality..43

Counseling Session 4: A Deeper Understanding.........47
Some Failure is Normal 48
The Story of Bobby..49
Unleashing the Power of Prayer 51
What Does Satan Want? 52
Conquering Baseless or Unreasonable Fear and Anxiety 55
The Pain of Healing 56
Perfect Sex: In the Garden of Eden 59
The Peach and the Candy Bar 60
Shattered World 63
Beyond Sex and Sensuality—A Spiritual Model.....................65
Seeking Restoration 69
A Very Personal Example.......................................71
More on God as Our Lover: A Supernatural Vision 74
Eroticism is for Now 75
Perfect Peace...77

Counseling Session 5: Anger Management.............81
Case Study in Betrayal & Anger Management: The Story of A..........85
Transforming Anger & Hurt 87
Moving Beyond the Incident with A 90
The Secret to Super-Charged Healing: Reasoning Faith................91
Applying the Joshua Protocol to the Case of A......................93

Counseling Session 6: Experiencing Change............ 99
The Bible is But a Single Word 100
The Significance of the Joshua Protocol 102
On Forgiveness..102
Attempt Reconciliation 105
Achieving Shalom 106
Transformation is All About Taking Control 107
Pray for Others 109
Story of The Little Red Lizard 111
Is Change Happening in Me?....................................114
Threat of Relapse 116

Conclusion: A Better Tomorrow 119
The Defeat of Evil..122

Appendix 1: Additional Applications 125
The Joshua Protocol for Obsessive-Compulsive Disorder (OCD) 126
The Joshua Protocol for Overcoming Low Self-Esteem 126
The Joshua Protocol for Overcoming a Poor Attitude. 127
The Joshua Protocol for Overcoming Laziness. 127
The Joshua Protocol for Overcoming Procrastination. 128
The Joshua Protocol for Overcoming Gossip. 128
The Joshua Protocol for Overcoming Sadness. 129
The Joshua Protocol for Stealing 129
The Joshua Protocol for Liars 130
The Joshua Protocol for Post-Traumatic Stress Disorder (PTSD) 131
The Joshua Protocol for Excessive Preoccupation with Entertainment. 131
The Joshua Protocol for Unwarranted Fear and Anxiety 132
The Joshua Protocol for Gambling Addiction 132
The Joshua Protocol for Compulsive, Emotional, or Out-of-Control
    Spending 133
The Joshua Protocol for Overcoming Pride or Arrogance. 133
The Joshua Protocol for Overcoming Hurtful Sarcasm. 134
The Joshua Protocol for Overcoming Jealousy or Envy 135
The Joshua Protocol for Overcoming Greed 135
The Joshua Protocol for Overcoming Selfishness 136
The Joshua Protocol for Overcoming Hoarding Behaviors 136
The Joshua Protocol for Overcoming Drug Abuse 137
The Joshua Protocol for Overcoming Alcohol Abuse 137
The Joshua Protocol to Stop Smoking. 138

Appendix 2: Scriptural References. 141
Bible Passages for Better Thought Control 141
Bible Passages for Overcoming Negativity and Pessimism. 150

Endnotes 163
Bibliography 171
Index 175

Introduction

This book is a gift. I am more of a spokesperson, and not so much an author. Let me warn you, from the beginning, that the ideas presented herein might seem "too good to be true" for some people. Please do not shoot the messenger as you read this account of my real-life experiences. This is my personal story. It really happened. Moreover, I believe this book has the potential to help a vast audience; this is why I am offering such a detailed account of what I have learned. I hope this work will be useful to you, the reader, or to someone you know who is hurting in their emotions and can benefit from the lessons that follow.

I am a child abuse survivor. As a youngster growing up, I lived through a series of painful life experiences that involved physical, emotional, and even sexual abuse. Most of these life events took place when I was between the ages of five and twelve years old. For the next forty years, I carried psychological and emotional scars to include low self-esteem, as well as built-up anger and resentment. Additionally, I developed an assortment of bad habits, all of which were linked to those difficult early years of my life. I had never sought professional help to address my past experiences until I reached the age of fifty. At that time, a friend told me about an amazing Christian therapist whom he described as both affable and knowledgeable. I soon scheduled an appointment to meet a man whom I will call *the Counselor*.

A distinguished older gentleman in his seventies, the

Counselor worked as a licensed marriage and family therapist with offices in California. He ran a comfortable practice out of a professional building located in an upscale suburb of a major city. When I first met my new therapist, I noted his casual demeanor. The Counselor was a tall, soft-spoken, thin man. He wore casual, open-collared shirts and sweaters that helped give our interactions a feeling of informality. His office, where all our conversations took place, was neatly appointed with an overstuffed couch, a pair of comfortable chairs, and a small wooden office desk in the corner. There were tasteful and attractive knick-knacks and decorative items strewn throughout the room, all of which served to give the space a homey and comfortable feel. The exterior windows of the office were over-sized and allowed for an abundance of natural light and unobstructed views of the neatly landscaped grounds that surrounded the professional building. It was not long until I started to feel at ease in such a relaxing and peaceful environment. I later began to look forward to my counseling sessions, as the Counselor's office came to symbolize for me a welcome respite from the hectic challenges of the outside world.

During our initial introductions, the Counselor told me he was a long-practicing Christian who had attended seminary and had been an American Baptist minister. He served for twenty-two years as a naval chaplain, and his educational background included seven university degrees, two of which were Ph.Ds.[1] Much later in our relationship, he shared with me that our sessions were especially "fun" for him because he could leverage his seminary background and use his knowledge of spiritual concepts to enhance my therapy sessions. The Counselor said most of his other patients were secularistic, non-Christians. For them, he used a strictly "medical model" for treatment that entailed methods drawn from modern psychology, without any integration or reference to God or spirituality.

I attended a total of six, one-hour counseling sessions with this amazing teacher. All six meetings took place over a four-month period. The experience, for me, was life-changing. The depth and breadth of my new therapist's knowledge both amazed and overwhelmed me, beginning from our very first hour together. The format of my counseling sessions had me asking the therapist a series of questions and then listening intently to his responses. This was unlike some other counseling approaches, whereby a therapist might typically ask a patient a series of questions to try and elicit meanings and answers to problems. My sessions were different in that the Counselor told me flatly: "You run the sessions. I am as a guest in my own office. You tell me the direction you want us to take." The responses to the questions I posed became more like the best kind of college seminars. It was like listening to a seasoned university professor speaking at length while drawing, not from notes, but from his own vast experience, intellect, research, and general knowledge.

To be honest, when we first started our professional client-therapist relationship, I was somewhat suspicious of my new mentor. The Counselor presented a variety of concepts and ideas that were new and foreign to me. I independently researched the names and resources the Counselor cited during our first few therapy sessions. The scholarly authorities he referenced, as well as the principles presented from the fields of psychology and human brain research, all checked out as genuine. My trust in my new therapist quickly grew. Moreover, the amount of detailed information the Counselor presented, made me feel like I was drinking water from a raging fire hose. The richness and depth of our interactions prompted me to soon make a special request: I asked permission to use a digital voice recorder to capture the information the Counselor was providing to me during my sessions. My new therapist paused for a moment. He then cautiously consented, saying that such a request was unusual and that he had never before allowed a patient to record their therapy sessions. But the Counselor understood I wanted to use the audio recordings of our discussions for subsequent review; he saw I was intent on getting the maximum benefit from our talks. In the end, it was from those original voice recordings that I wrote the majority of this book.

My time with the Counselor passed quickly, and I began to see positive results within a couple of months. The initial focus of my treatment had to do with confronting memories of childhood physical and sexual abuse. I learned that many of my adult behaviors and attitudes stemmed from a series of tumultuous events from my past. I came to understand how the life narrative of my youth later positioned me to feel low self-esteem, jealousy, lust, anger, pride, and a variety of other repetitive and compulsive emotions. My bad adult habits were caused by hurtful or otherwise damaging episodes from early in life. For example, by age five, I had been sexually exploited by others. Furthermore, my first exposure to pornography was at the age of twelve. Once I began therapy, I soon understood that I had been mentally trained or "programmed" in certain ways of thinking as a result of my early life experiences. When I finally sought professional help, as a middle-aged man, I desperately wanted to be set free from an unhealthy world of fantasy and destructive habits, many of which centered around the topics of anger and sexuality. But more importantly, I came to understand that what I was learning could be adapted to help other people who suffer from a variety of psychological challenges and emotional pains. I was almost dumbfounded by the seemingly global applications for the information that the Counselor presented to me. As far as I could tell, many kinds of emotional hurt and suffering could be addressed and made better through a biblically-based process, which the Counselor called the *Joshua Protocol*.

During my treatment, I tried doing research but could find no information or reference to any Joshua Protocol. I finally confronted the Counselor, at my final therapy session, and asked him where he had gotten his information about this powerful tool. His response was one of mild amusement, after which he told me the Joshua Protocol was a result of his intensive research and study of the Old and New Testaments of the Bible. He then went on to explain how his seminary training, combined with his understanding of the Hebrew language, allowed him to conduct a thorough analysis of the biblical story of Joshua. From his extensive scholarly work, he successfully distilled and unveiled deep meanings from within the ancient texts. The Counselor told me the lessons he had extracted from the Old Testament writings were, to his thinking, "explicit" and obvious in both their power and current application. He argued that, in antiquity, the Old Testament Jews of the Bible had been tested in much the same manner as people are still being tested today. Therefore, the Counselor reasoned that the lessons he found in the book of Joshua offer value and relevance for us now. Later, I will deliver a step-by-step presentation that outlines how anyone can use the Joshua Protocol.

I was also reminded that we who live in contemporary society enjoy advantages that were not available to those portrayed in the Bible. Scientific discoveries, combined with a better understanding of human consciousness, have significantly changed the face of psychology and the field of mental health. The discussion that follows in this book consists of a fascinating blend of contemporary neuroscience and religious faith. For example, we will consider how we can make changes and improvements to the human brain. We will also discuss the difference between "the mind" and "the brain." Ultimately, I learned during counseling that my goal should be to grow my spiritual mind, which is physically housed within the apparatus I refer to as my brain. I came to understand that by seeking positive brain change and spiritual development, it was possible for me to displace harmful behaviors. Moreover, I could build healthier thinking patterns and instill better habits.

At the end of four months, my course of therapy was over. The Counselor heartily congratulated me, saying: "Eric, I have never in my life seen anybody get so much out of six sessions." In truth, I had been given some powerful knowledge that I quickly began to leverage in order to address the painful events of my childhood. But I also felt somewhat like an archaeological explorer who had stumbled upon a magical Fountain of Youth or some other dramatic discovery. I became strangely uneasy with the knowledge I had gained. The concepts I learned from the biblical teachings seemed too big and important to withhold from the rest of the world. The need to share the information started to weigh upon me. In my final therapy session, I felt compelled to confront the Counselor.

ERIC: "Have you written a book about all of this?"

THE COUNSELOR: "No, I've just done doctoral dissertations and papers. In the past, I started writing a few books, but never felt led to finish one. I might someday. I have been encouraged to promote my work using the mass media, and also to teach graduate courses, but I like what I am doing here with my private practice."

ERIC: "Honestly, I am a little bit concerned, because what would happen to all this valuable information if you, for example, got killed in an accident, or otherwise died tomorrow?"

THE COUNSELOR: "I am not worried. I am just an expression of God's consciousness. God's consciousness does not die. I am serving the purpose for which I am called. And until God tells me to write books or move to Hollywood, as some people have suggested I should, I'm not doing it. I don't need it. I don't want it. I am content here. I have joy."

ERIC: "What if you had somebody else write the book and be the public face for sharing the information with the world? You could remain behind-the-scenes. You could operate in the shadows and stay invisible."

THE COUNSELOR: "Write the book yourself. You have found something special in this. You have been given a treasure, and it belongs to you. You be the steward of it. You may use the knowledge, and you may even sell it if you'd like. You own this product, and you don't have a partner, except God. You have my blessing."

I walked out of the professional office for the last time, feeling slightly dazed and confused. What had just happened? I felt an obligation to share all the authentic, innovative, and compelling information that the Counselor gifted to me. This information was unique, and few others in the world knew about it. Did God want *me* to write a book and communicate these concepts? I am not a university professor, a therapist, or a professional theologian. Yet, the Counselor had taught me an effective system that can empower people to address a broad range of emotional dysfunction and human suffering. This new tool, the Joshua Protocol, offers fresh hope to those who suffer from a variety of serious life challenges, including:

- Threats to personal purity and moral integrity, such as pornography, inappropriate thoughts, fantasy, or other negative behaviors associated with human sexuality.
- Anger from emotional and physical hurt or betrayal.
- Obsessive-Compulsive Disorder (OCD).

- Low self-esteem, emotional insecurity, poor attitude, or persistent sadness.
- Unwarranted fear and anxiety.
- Selfishness, jealousy, or envy.
- Laziness or procrastination.
- Gossip, hurtful sarcasm, pride, or arrogance.
- Greed, gambling addiction, or compulsivity with money.
- Obsessive preoccupation with entertainment, social media, or electronic gaming.
- Hoarding behaviors.
- Substance abuse (alcohol, tobacco, or other drugs).

The title of this book, *Stop Resisting Your Sins!*, requires some explanation. The title speaks to a fundamental truth found in the Bible. Since the fall of Adam and Eve in the Garden of Eden, humanity has proven itself to be clumsy and largely unsuccessful in *resisting* behaviors and activities that are unhealthy. Jesus, himself, witnessed the physical limitations of his apostles in the Garden of Gethsemane. Jesus asked his twelve closest friends to remain alert and by his side during the tumultuous hours before Jesus' arrest and subsequent murder. But despite their best intentions and efforts, the Twelve Disciples kept falling asleep at precisely the time Jesus needed them most. Jesus commented on the fate of the human condition when he concluded, "the spirit is willing, but the flesh is weak."[2]

Moreover, in his fantasy novel, *The Screwtape Letters*, Irish writer and scholar C.S. Lewis describes the peculiar hybrid nature of humanity. Lewis tells us, "Humans are amphibians—half spirit and half animal."[3] The body-and-flesh connection to the higher consciousness often leads to inappropriate choices and significant ethical failures. Too often the body's lower nature overwhelms the better tendencies of the human spirit.

Consider the problem of a person's addiction to alcohol. A determined recovering alcoholic may, for many years, participate successfully in a Twelve-Step Program. The recovering alcoholic may even enjoy extended periods of perfect sobriety, so long as he or she can resist the temptation to consume alcohol. But, at some point, it is not unusual for a recovering alcoholic to experience a "break" in his or her sobriety, whereby the alcoholic succumbs to the temptation to drink.

Dieting and exercise programs provide additional examples of how well-intentioned people attempt to use sheer willpower and human effort to make positive life changes. The so-called "Yo-Yo Diet" phenomenon showcases how inner strength and willpower fades, and how the temptations of life can become too strong and overwhelming for people to resist. The remaining pages of this book will argue that the secret for successful living comes, not from invoking our own "inner strength," and not by successfully *resisting* our negative impulses. Instead, we will propose that significant life changes can be brought about by *transforming* negative human impulses into something positive and beautiful—God worship.

There is an interesting passage in the Bible that helps to illustrate this idea of changing something bad into something good. In 1 Samuel 21:9 (NIV), there is a story of how David was being pursued by his enemies who were eager to kill him. The biblical passage tells how David was in desperate need of a weapon that he could use to defend himself. He sought the help of a priest, who, as luck would have it, was in possession of a very special sword. The priest told David:

> "The sword of Goliath the Philistine, whom you killed in the Valley of Elah, is here; it is wrapped in a cloth behind the ephod. If you want it, take it."

> David said, "There is none like it; give it to me."

Notice how David gained control over a savage weapon that initially had been intended to destroy *him*. The story of David and Goliath is told in 1 Samuel 17. The Bible recounts the narrative of a battle whereby David kills the mighty warrior Goliath, using just a sling and a stone. This first illustration establishes what will become an essential theme for the remainder of this book. Namely, that people can take control of "the bad things of life" and use those difficult life experiences to build a better future for themselves. In other words, this book is about learning skills for changing *bad* life experiences into something *good*.

But before we begin, there is one last piece of housekeeping. In my writing, I often use the word *sin*. I admit the term carries plenty of baggage with it. While many readers of this work will firmly identify themselves as "Christians," there will likely be others who have no religious affiliation whatsoever. Non-Christian readers may be evaluating this book in the hope of finding a powerful approach to dealing with their bad habits and life struggles. Clearly, Christians will be more familiar (and maybe even *comfortable?*) with the term "sin" and its various connotations. But for any non-Christians reading this text, please consider the term "sin" as a form of shorthand, or as a writer's convenience.

For non-Christian audiences, I could, perhaps, have talked about life challenges, poor personal "choices," or poor "decision making." I could also have substituted a long and cumbersome list of other nouns such as "dysfunction," "difficulty," "compulsion," "fixation," or "obsession," to effectively communicate some of the appropriate meanings. But clearly, individuals suffering the effects of depression, obsessive-compulsive disorder, or who suffered violence or child abuse or other similar circumstances, all deserve compassion and support. It is not my intent to shame, blame, or label anyone as a "bad person," or to make anyone feel unworthy or worthless. For our purposes here, we will neither accuse nor pass judgments regarding current or past behaviors or habits. Instead, we will assume that everyone faces their own challenges, hang-ups, shortcomings, or is somehow dealing with their own brand of sickness or—sin.

Lastly, I hope that this work will help a diverse group of people from all races, backgrounds, beliefs, and sexual orientations. Everyone is welcome to benefit from the potent insights that follow. However, for the sake of streamlining this book and to keep it brief and easily readable, I will write using mostly masculine pronouns, in a style that might make it first appear to be a book written solely for a straight, male audience. But feel free to adjust the written words, in your thinking, and adapt this information to meet *your* needs.

Given all of this as background, let us now look in the following chapter at our understanding of the human brain. For starters, we will consider how environmental conditioning impacts human behavior.

Review of the Introduction

1. Our life experiences play an important role in shaping our thinking and our behavior. This is particularly true of events that take place early in our lives as children.
2. There is a war being waged within each of us. It is a conflict between our animalistic instincts and our higher spiritual consciousness.
3. By itself, sheer human willpower will almost always fail when it comes to resisting negative thinking and destructive emotional impulses.
4. We must learn how to change negative thought processes into positive actions. Our hope for the future comes from knowing that good results can come from bad beginnings.
5. We must learn how to *transform* evil into good.

Counseling Session 1
Basic Principles

The Counselor began our first session by giving me some important background information and useful definitions. He told me there has been a revolution in the field of brain science and psychology. In the past, there had been no recognized difference between the human *brain* and the *self*. But research by Rudolph "Rudy" Tanzi, a professor of neurology, at Harvard Medical School, has revealed we are no longer our brains—we each just have a brain. He says that we are, in fact, our minds, or our consciousness. Moreover, while the following illustration may not be ideal, I started to better understand these ideas when I compared the human brain to a computer. A computer's hardware data storage capability can be configured and reconfigured using a software application. Similarly, the human mind or consciousness may be thought of as the "software" that can reconfigure the physical "hardware" apparatus we call the brain. The main point is that the brain is not a fixed or "hardwired" object, but instead, it can be reformatted, remapped, or otherwise reprogrammed. Over time, the brain can be rendered better or worse; the choice is ours. Ultimately, we can gain more effective control over how the brain matures and develops—if we can master the lessons taught in this text.

Dr. Tanzi co-wrote a book, entitled *Super Brain*, with Deepak Chopra. In his book, Dr. Tanzi describes how something called *neuroplasticity* gives every person the ability to change the physical structure of his or her brain. This fact is important for people who possess deep emotional wounds from their past life experiences. As I like to think of it, neuroplasticity is a fancy word that simply means "brain change."[4] Moreover, while the concept of neuroplasticity is not new, it offers people hope to repair the damage that results from their hurtful emotional pasts.[5] It is important that individuals attend to their old traumas or memories of pain. Unaddressed emotional wounds can prompt negative behaviors that may adversely influence a person's quality of life and future success. With an understanding of neuroplasticity, Dr. Tanzi and many other professionals in the mental health community believe that the human brain can be reshaped, and its functionality improved.[6] We can fashion a healthier, better brain by introducing positive habits to replace negative ones. The remainder of this book will focus on techniques and suggestions for promoting positive brain change.

During my therapy sessions, the Counselor seemed to enjoy taking unexpected little tangents in the middle of our discussions. We would be talking about one subject or another, and then, without warning, he would suddenly divert in a new and unexpected direction. I needed to pay close attention during our time spent together. Otherwise, he would quickly leave me behind when he abruptly changed subjects. For example, as we were discussing the topic of neuroplasticity, the Counselor interjected his opinion that people should blend ideas taken from science and medicine into their spiritual growth and development. He felt uneasy about how some Christian people seem to shun science in favor of purely faith-based approaches to life. But he insisted that God created both science and medicine, and these two things are given to everyone equally.

Overcoming Human Nature

In the Bible, Galatians 2:20 (ESV) teaches that Christian people have been spiritually "crucified" along with Jesus Christ. The apostle Paul says, "It is no longer I who live, but Christ who lives in me." The idea is that Christians today have the Spirit of God within them, through something called the indwelling of the Holy Spirit. A goal of Christianity is to raise this godly presence up into the higher consciousness of everyone who claims to embrace the Christian lifestyle. Once God inhabits and becomes a part of a person's everyday life, the individual can then begin to live and make decisions that are consistent with Jesus Christ's superior character, values, and example. By contrast, many people follow the pattern set by our fallen popular culture. They make their life decisions based upon the character and contemporary values of society. For them, the results can prove poisonous to their lives.

The process of becoming more Christlike and for adopting a healthier, godlier lifestyle, is far from easy. This is because the physical brain becomes filled with harsh memories and experiences from our pasts. This unfortunate reality makes it hard for Christians to live like Jesus did. The solution is that we must mentally go to war against any corrupt values we may hold, and ultimately subdue them. Only when our higher-level thinking overwhelms our animalistic instincts, will we be positioned to achieve our real potential and become the people we were meant to be. Moreover, our enhanced ability to make better choices will result in our living new and more positive lives.

For four hundred years, the mainstream scientific community saw the human brain as a machine with parts that could not be fixed once damaged.[7] For centuries, it was believed that people's mental or emotional health problems could only be "managed" and "lived with" or masked using drugs. But the good news is that Dr. Tanzi now tells us the human brain is "plastic" or changeable. Furthermore, by shifting the way we think in our higher consciousness, we have the power to subdue the brain and make it perform in a positive manner—in any manner we choose. Dr. Tanzi writes, "It's hard to really absorb that every thought is an instruction [to the brain], but it is."[8]

This means we can "rewire" the physical structure and workings of the brain. The functional pathways associated with our bad habits can be rerouted into new and more healthful ways of thinking and behaving. Consider your brain as an appliance that can be upgraded. We may literally command the brain to change and to improve. The field of psychology and mental health now embraces the notion that we have the option to take control of our mental processes, and that fundamental and significant change is possible within the human brain. This improved understanding represents a revolution of greater hope for those who currently experience destructive behavioral or emotional patterns, or out-of-control compulsions or bad habits.

The Human Brain—Made Simple

Before we go much further, I want to offer a simplified model of the human brain. This easy to understand representation was given to me by the Counselor during my therapy visits, and it is how we will refer to the brain during the remainder of this book. In truth, the human brain is anything but simple, and the model I am now presenting has its limitations. But, for our purposes, let us just say the human brain is made up of two physical parts. Moreover, let us name those two parts the *lower brain* and the *upper brain*. Imagine that the lower region of the brain holds our "primal" instincts. The word, *primal*, comes from the Latin root *primus*, which simply means "first" or "early." The lower brain develops early in a person's life, and it is designed to deal with basic survival issues. For example, the primal brain regulates our essential bodily functions such as heart rate, breathing, and swallowing. It also prompts our so-called "fight or flight" survival response. Additionally, the lower brain triggers a desire to eat food and is also responsible for sexual urges, many of a person's emotions, and other instinctual behaviors.

MODEL 1
THE HUMAN BRAIN
GREATLY SIMPLIFIED INTO TWO PARTS

1. TERMINOLOGY AND FUNCTIONS ASSOCIATED WITH THE UPPER BRAIN:
- THE MIND / THE INTELLECT / THE HIGHER CONSCIOUSNESS
- HIGHER ORDER THINKING & REASONING / THE CAPACITY FOR CHOICE
- WHERE THE HUMAN "SPIRIT" RESIDES

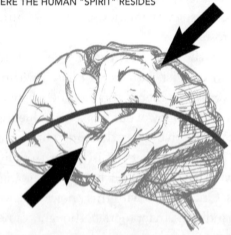

2. TERMINOLOGY AND FUNCTIONS ASSOCIATED WITH THE LOWER BRAIN:
- THE PRIMAL EMOTIONS AND INSTINCTS
- HUNGER & SEXUAL APPETITES
- THE "FIGHT OR FLIGHT" SURVIVAL RESPONSE
- WHERE BREATHING, SWALLOWING, AND HEART RATE ARE REGULATED

By contrast, it is within the upper half of the human brain that the function of the "mind" resides. The mind represents an individual's awareness of his or her own existence and allows people to achieve higher levels of thinking. Furthermore, the mind lends the ability to define and establish a person's convictions and ethical values. There are other similar words I may use interchangeably to express the same meaning as the "mind." These other similar terms include the "higher consciousness," "intellect," "executive function," and the "human spirit." But the main point is that, according to our model, the mind is physically housed within the upper half of the human brain. Moreover, the mind is what separates humanity from the many other species of life that inhabit the earth. It is from this amazing realm of the upper brain that art, literature, poetry, ethics, religion, spirituality, philosophy, philanthropy, politics, mathematics, science, engineering, and technology all arose.

Unfortunately, the functions that reside within the upper brain are often in conflict with those housed within the lower brain. In other words, our higher consciousness fights against our basic, primal instincts. Many of our problems in life stem from the hard-to-control, instinctive urges that originate from the lower brain. It is like each of us has two distinct personalities fighting for control of who we are. We all have an ongoing war being waged within us. Once armed with this knowledge, we can better recognize and handle the inappropriate thoughts or negativity we experience. For example, whenever we have a wrong thought or an unhealthy emotion, our upper brain can honestly say, *"It's not me."*

Most unhealthy patterns do not originate from the upper brain's "higher-consciousness." Instead, most of our bad habits come from the lower brain's past life experience and conditioning. Such toxic life narrative is lodged deeply within our primal thinking. The negativity is tied to our physicality, our flesh, our environment, and our past social interactions. These things are not consistent with our higher, ethical, intellectual, or spiritual selves. Our negativity comes out of our lower-brain experiences, but we are not our lower brains. Moreover, we can correctly and immediately reject any unhealthy or self-destructive thinking, without accepting shame, guilt, or feelings of regret for such thoughts.

Let me quickly add that *people are still responsible for their actions*. It would be foolishness to engage in inappropriate, self-destructive, or illegal behavior, only to subsequently try and deny accountability by pointing to primal compulsions as an excuse for bad behavior. That simply will not work. Consider the prison systems that detain individuals who may have allowed their primal brains to disproportionately influence their actions. None of those incarcerated persons have escaped the painful justice imposed by society. The basic warning here is that we must learn to have our higher consciousness firmly dominate and control the primal brain. But achieving this goal is easier said than done. The apostle Paul wrote about this very subject in the New Testament. Paul, who was a devout, God-worshipping man, struggled with inner turmoil and conflict during the time of his Christian ministry.[9] At one point, in his writings to the Roman people, Paul confessed flatly:

> I do not understand my own actions. For I do not do what I want, but I do the very thing I hate. Now if I do what I do not want, it is no longer I who do it, but sin that dwells within me.[10]

In the above passage, Paul confesses his own weakness. He called it *sin*. But what is most intriguing is how he suggests that there are two conflicting forces at odds within him. In fact, Paul is correct. But the "sin" to which Paul refers, is not really him. Paul goes so far as to say: "It is no longer I who do it." What Paul appears to be describing is his higher consciousness viciously fighting against his lower nature. Just as we do today, Paul had both a lower and upper brain. And just as we do today, Paul struggled with an inner dichotomy of opposing thoughts, feelings, and appetites.

Human beings are intended to be more than mere animals. In God's estimation, we are something grander—we are a higher consciousness; we are spirit-based creatures who resemble God, Himself.[11] A goal of Christianity is for individuals to surrender their physical and psychological being over to the greater will of the creator of the universe. Together, as humanity, we are supposed to serve as what is known in the Bible as "the body of Christ." We are the physical beings through which God's life and consciousness can become tangible on earth. Paul went on to explain this in his other writings:

> I have been crucified with Christ and I no longer live, but Christ lives in me. The life I now live in the body, I live by faith in the Son of God, who loved me and gave himself for me.[12]

Paul spoke the same way about other people, saying to the multitudes, "Now you are the body of Christ, and each one of you is a part of it."[13]

In sum, Christians are supposed to function as the ambassadors of God on earth.[14] We are supposed to act as the physical "hands and feet" of the spiritual Lord of the universe. Unfortunately, we do not always fulfill God's hopes and purposes. What I will term as "junk" gets in our way. By junk, I am talking about all the dysfunctions, hurts, disappointments, violence, chaos, and other disruptive narrative that other people and society use to overwhelm us. It is easy to understand why we might lose touch with our true identity as the much-beloved children of an all-powerful, infinite, God.

An Illustration: You Versus *Not* You

The Counselor gave me an example of how all of this works. Imagine if you found out that you had a cancerous tumor in your body. It would be silly to say to yourself, "I am cancer; I am a tumor." The cancerous tumor does not define who you are. Cancer is not your identity. Similarly, your body periodically does unpleasant things (e.g., burping, vomiting, flatulating, defecating, etc.) that are tied to biology and to the fact that we live in a physical universe. But despite these physical realities—you are not a burp or vomit. Neither are you a fart nor excrement. In the same way, we need to stop believing we are our bad habits or our sins. Dysfunction does not define us. Sin is not who we are. Sin is not our identity. On the contrary, God loves all of His creation and all of His people. *God loves you.* Furthermore, those who have chosen to embrace the Christian lifestyle have been completely *forgiven* of their sins and stand in perfect wholeness before God as joint heirs with Jesus Christ.[15]

Know the difference between "you" and "not you." The sin is "not you." Sin does not ultimately define your core character or who you are intrinsically. Sin is merely an unfortunate attitudinal or behavioral expression that can often become visible to society through your decisions and actions. The Counselor told me sin is like an invading virus or bacteria. We need to combat such "infections." We must not let such infections go unchecked to take hold and grow within us. When attacked by sin, we must rally quickly by believing that we are loved by God and have value in His eyes. Sin is real, but it does not belong to us. Consider yourself dead to sin and alive to God through the death and self-sacrifice of Jesus Christ.[16] Bad memories can give you unhealthy desires for things that you should not want. Bad memories are infectious thoughts. The uglier these thoughts, the greater their power. Such bad memories, along with their associated false beliefs and sick desires, are dangerous.

The Counselor went on to say, "You need something that grounds you and lets you discern what is you, and what is not you." Once you know who you are, that is, once you become aware of your higher consciousness and purpose, you can then delve into your lower brain and cleanse it of infectious thoughts and bad desires. Christians have Jesus Christ as a role model. By reading the biblical stories about Jesus, people can see examples of how a fully healthy, mature, and completely self-actualized person once lived. Moreover, if we today develop our faith in Christ and adopt the lifestyle of Christianity, then we quickly learn that Jesus lives within us. All of Jesus is in Christians and Christians believe that Jesus is God.[17] And when we have God in us, He strengthens us.

On The Topic of Evil

Christian psychiatrist, Morgan Scott Peck, wrote a pair of interesting books on the subject of demonology: *Glimpses of the Devil* and also *People of the Lie*. But the truth is all of us in society have accumulated lots of bad life experiences, either from our culture or from our family situations. The Counselor told me the main source of people's problems, both today and in the past, has been primarily worldly and secular, and only rarely Satanic or demonic. Additionally, some symptoms of mental illness, drug addiction, or other factors can mimic demonic possession in humans. And though we are certainly subjected to evil spiritual influences today, the Counselor said, "It is uncommon to see legitimate demonic possession of persons in modern, industrialized countries." Today, Satan and his demons can attack us by planting negative thoughts into our brains. But the Counselor told me that I would be wise to visit countries in Africa, or perhaps the Caribbean nation of Haiti, to find examples of full-blown demonic possession of humans, the kind of which has been popularized in classic Hollywood movies like *The Exorcist*.[18]

The Counselor went on to say, "But wicked acts against children are real." Moreover, the memories put into children are carried forward into adulthood. These memories must be transformed, and the evil must be separated from the victim. The correct approach is similar to how a caterpillar changes into a beautiful butterfly, or how a grain of sand in an oyster is fashioned into a precious pearl. The victim must not ignore the negative thoughts that enter him or her; otherwise, this thinking will grow and ultimately consume the person. Instead, the victim must attack the negative thoughts and change them into something better. The Bible instructs us that those who are "most eager" can achieve God's kingdom using "forceful action."[19]

The Counselor warned that victims of abuse and violence must replace negative thoughts with positive thoughts. The idea is to overwhelm the bad experiences of life with an abundance of God's mercy, love, and forgiveness. Here, we are not advocating repression of negativity, but rather its destruction. The aim is to destroy any thoughts that are negative or otherwise "sick." Tell yourself: *"This thought is not me. It is like an infection."* Once you have made this declaration in your mind, move forward and feel and experience the beauty of life. The goal is to convert all the negative experiences and emotions of life into something good. Repression, or otherwise choosing not to face and deal with bad thoughts, bad habits, or past hurts, does not work. Repression of negativity only allows the negativity to grow. You must force yourself to face the evil, deal with the hurtful narrative of life, and change all the negativity into something positive.

For the purposes of this book, *prayer* and *meditation* together will form the recommended approach for bringing about emotional and psychological healing. *Prayer* is a kind of communication that binds us to God. Prayer is a relational connection that unleashes the Lord's heavenly resources so we may be healed from our broken state of existence. We cannot restore ourselves, but must look to a Higher Power to transform us and produce greater health and wholeness. We must quickly take our problems to God and then depend on Him to lead us in resolving our life challenges.

Meditate on the Bible

The Counselor encouraged me to meditate on biblical Scriptures. He said I should practice mentally slowing myself down as I read the texts. He argued against quickly skimming or mindlessly reciting the chapters and verses of the Bible. He said such robotic rituals are of limited value. Instead, people should try to achieve a richer understanding of God's Word. Memorization of short biblical verses is an okay place to start, but then we should move deeper by meditating on the Scriptures. *Meditation* means to study, explore, and carefully consider and think about what the written words are really saying. When you read a verse in the Bible, stop and reflect upon what each word tells you. Give God a chance to speak His truth into your open mind and heart.

Try going online to discover what those biblical words and phrases mean in their original Hebrew or Greek translations. Then look at the Bible chapters and verses that both precede and follow the Scripture you are studying. Consider the broader context into which a particular Scripture falls. Perform a search and critically read the available online "biblical commentaries" of experts who offer additional perspectives on a Scriptural passage that is of interest to you. Take some time to ponder over what you discover as you study and learn about the Bible. Do not rush through the process. Your spiritual growth and development is more like a marathon than it is a sprinter's race. It can be a highly rewarding process that will take you a lifetime. Do not be in a hurry, but instead, learn to enjoy the spiritual journey.

The Counselor then showed me a simple mental exercise I could do. As an example, he asked me to think about what the Bible might mean by the word "good." He then walked me through a brief contemplation exercise that began to model for me the process of meditation. Thinking aloud, he asked himself the following questions:

> Have I ever seen "good" in action?

> Have I ever seen a transformation of something bad into something good?

How can I make things good? I, myself, don't have the power to make things good. I had better go to God, who alone makes things good.

How do I feel about God making everything around me good?

I love it when God makes things turn out well!

A key point here is to underscore the fact that we should stay away from any over-reliance on repetitive or highly ritualistic activity that quickly loses its meaning. Instead, try to both educate and unfetter your mind and allow it the freedom to absorb and achieve a better understanding of God's Word as presented in the Bible. Give permission for the Holy Spirit to inspire your higher consciousness and make the biblical Scriptures come alive and become relevant to you. "That is how you can spiritually grow," the Counselor concluded.

Celebrate Everything and Transform Bad into Good

Celebrate, emotionally, the good things that happen in life. Celebrate even the small victories. Assign positive meanings to your experiences. Choose to be positive, even under unpleasant circumstances. The Counselor taught me you can shape and train your brain to be more positive and optimistic. Literally, you can change the functional pathways in your physical brain to reflect and be optimized to support a better outlook on life. Go from a negative to a positive worldview. In the biblical book of James, it says to "rejoice" when you face fiery trials.[20] At first, this may seem like complete nonsense. But we should consistently give thanks during tough times, so to neutralize the negative energy that life throws at us every day. In general, the hard work of the Christian is to re-think or re-author all the painful events that come our way and to, instead, change all the Good

Friday tragedies into Easter Sunday celebrations. Attempt to find new meanings during your struggles. What lessons can be learned? How can conflict and hardship make you a stronger person?

But maybe, right about now, you are thinking to yourself, "Yeah, but you don't know what I have been through in my life and what people have done to me. I have nothing to celebrate." I recall once having an interesting conversation with a Vietnam War veteran friend of mine. He told me about his wartime experiences as a soldier in the U.S. Army Infantry. He spoke of the hardships and the horrors of combat. Yet, in the midst of the uncertainty and the fear, he also recognized that he had been surrounded by tremendous natural beauty. In the face of uncertain battles and possible death, his senses became heightened, and he grew keenly aware of his physical surroundings. Moreover, he felt immense appreciation for the incredible beauty of the vast, lush, Vietnamese jungle that engulfed him. He spoke romantically and nostalgically about the mighty rivers and the stunning azure skies he experienced as a soldier. Even though he was surrounded by dangerous enemies and often thought he might die, he managed to feel many moments of joy as he encountered great natural splendor and experienced a strange peace that surpassed his understanding.[21] He summarized for me his experience by saying, "God's glory is always with you. It is there, somewhere, right in front of you. You just have to pay attention and see it."

Review of Counseling Session 1

1. Think of the human brain as an apparatus, an appliance, a platform, or a shell. The human self-awareness and the personal identity stored within the confines of the physical brain is much more important than the physical brain itself, which is merely a container or housing.
2. The apparatus we call the brain holds both our primal instincts and our higher consciousness. The higher consciousness is

sometimes called the mind or the intellect. In a religious context, this higher consciousness is often referred to as the human "spirit."
3. Our primal brains are essential to maintaining our safety and for regulating vital bodily functions. But this same lower, primal brain can also sometimes make us dysfunctional in our emotions, attitudes, and behaviors.
4. Almost as if there are two distinct personalities alive within each of us, the primal brain wars against the upper mind for control of a person's feelings and actions.
5. The secret to a better life is to have our minds and higher consciousness dominate over the animalistic instincts of our lower primal brains.
6. *Neuroplasticity* is a scientific term to describe the ability of the human brain to be reshaped and improved. A kind of "brain reprogramming" is possible whereby deeply held feelings and emotions, as well as deeply-rooted habits and behaviors, may be changed. Bad habits that have been "wired" into the brain can be transformed, and the brain's internal mapping improved. The result is that better attitudes and positive behavioral changes may be seen in individuals who have exhibited past bad habits.
7. Consistent prayer and meditation, as part of an ongoing practice of a Christian lifestyle, can transform the human brain in positive ways. The results may come in the form of a better life for those who embrace Christianity and establish a close personal relationship with God.

Counseling Session 2
Building a Relationship with God

The whole assembly grumbled against the leaders, but all the leaders answered, "We have given them our oath by the LORD, the God of Israel, and we cannot touch them now. This is what we will do to them: We will let them live, so that God's wrath will not fall on us for breaking the oath we swore to them." They continued, "Let them live, but let them be woodcutters and water carriers in the service of the whole assembly."

Joshua 9:19-21 (NIV)

The Gibeonite Deception

During my second therapy session with the Counselor, we started looking more deeply into the teachings of the Bible's Old Testament. The Counselor began by instructing me on how the book of Joshua contains obscure biblical treasures and concepts that are highly useful in helping a person to overcome their bad habits and negative thinking. He noted that *Joshua* is the same name as *Jesus* in Hebrew, and that the content in the book of Joshua symbolizes the impacts made upon humanity by both society and the devil.

For example, in chapter 9 of the book of Joshua, the Bible describes how the Israelite army's military victories over the cities of Jericho and Ai resulted in word quickly spreading across the entire region that there was a new super-power on the scene. People and nations throughout the land fell into fear and dread that they would soon face destruction at the hands of the Israelites and their supreme God. The nearby people of Gibeon became terrified by the prospect of their own annihilation at the hands of the Jews. But the leaders of Gibeon devised a scheme to save themselves and their citizens. Gibeon quickly sent a team of ambassadors to trick Joshua and the Israelites into entering a peace treaty.

According to the Bible, the Jewish people had been commanded by God to subdue and destroy all the inhabitants of the land of Canaan. But the Gibeonites falsely presented themselves to the Jews as people from a powerful and distant region. The Gibeonites flattered Joshua and the Israelites, appealing to their vanity and pride. Upon being seduced, the Israelites quickly and unwisely made a binding peace accord with the Gibeonites. The sin of Joshua and the Israelites was to allow themselves to fall prey to the tricks of their enemy and to embrace a binding peace treaty without first consulting with God in prayer.[22]

Inappropriate Relationships

This story of Joshua and the Jewish people illustrates a significant problem facing contemporary society. Too often, we are lured into inappropriate relationships or practices, only to later find ourselves trapped in them. A few examples of the kinds of relationships I am talking about include a drug addict's relationship with narcotics, or an alcoholic's relationship with liquor, or an adult's inappropriate involvement with a prostitute or with pornography. Unfortunately, it is too easy to succumb to the many addictive temptations that are so abundantly available in today's culture. Moreover, once a person engages in a toxic or otherwise destructive relationship, it is often difficult to extract oneself from the situation without there being lasting damage.

Joshua soon discovered he had been seduced and tricked by the people of Gibeon. In the end, Joshua was forced to keep his promise to the Gibeonites, and he allowed them to live. The Gibeonite ambassadors had successfully manipulated the Israelites, just like society and the devil work to deceive and exploit us today. And while there were permanent consequences to Joshua's mistake, God, nonetheless, later outsmarted the Gibeonites. The Gibeonites had saved their lives through deception and lies, but they ultimately became the slaves of the Jews. Furthermore, in an ironic twist, the Gibeonites became the slaves who would specifically "carry the water and cut the wood" of the Jews in support of the sacred Israelite religious ceremonies that took place in the Jewish Holy Tabernacle. This is a key point: The insidious deception of the Gibeonites was *transformed* into something good and useful—God worship. Specifically, the type of slavery the Gibeonites were placed into was the kind that directly supported the work of the Jewish priests and the sacred religious practices of the Israelites. The Gibeonites were brought to their knees and forced to perform harsh labor that served to glorify and worship God.

A Special Prayer

The Counselor used the story of Joshua and the Gibeonites as an illustration of how "bad" life events can be transformed into "good" life outcomes. He went on to tell me about a bold and new therapeutic tool he had developed for use by his clients. He called it the Joshua Protocol. The Counselor extracted this healing process from the story of Joshua and the Gibeonites, and it parallels how the Israelite people achieved victory over the Gibeonite lie.

Briefly, the Joshua Protocol depends both upon the power of prayer and in maintaining a faithful commitment to a healing process. If you agree to encounter God and pray in the manner that I am about to describe, you can significantly reduce the impact of the hurtful aspects of your past. Moreover, you can refocus and alter the future direction of your life and defeat Satan's plan to ruin your tomorrows. Over time, you can replace the memories and effects of your "bad" life history with a more positive "good" future consisting of healthier habits, attitudes, and behaviors. You can achieve greater freedom from your compulsive or negative thoughts and actions by following the step-by-step biblical and spiritual prescription of the Joshua Protocol. This suggested Christian approach to behavior modification consists of three parts.

Seek Forgiveness

Firstly, the Counselor instructed me to symbolically and mentally see myself "approaching the Jewish altar," as I enter my personal prayer times with God. Jesus Christ was a Jew, and I have already mentioned how the same Hebrew word is used for both the names of Jesus and Joshua. Jesus today serves as the bridge that binds together the lessons of the Old Testament of the Jewish people, and the New Testament of the Christian faith. For a Christian, the symbolic altar represents the person of Christ. In my mind's eye, at the start of my personal prayer time, the Counselor encouraged me to see myself approaching Jesus and thanking him and his heavenly Father for the *forgiveness* of my sins. When we approach God and ask Him to forgive our sins, we engage in a kind of cleansing ceremony. This type of spiritual cleansing is symbolic of the same ritual washing that the Jewish priests undertook before worship, during the time of Joshua.

Our mistakes and bad habits—our sins—can be viewed as the symbolic "water and wood," or a kind of holy offering that is consumed by God whenever we pray. In this case, the word *wood* represents any substance that can be transformed from one state of being into another to release energy to accomplish work or a task. This is how we can be forgiven of our sins: We should express genuine regret and then offer all our "badness" to God during prayer. Our confessed badness becomes the symbolic wood that gets burned-up and destroyed during our prayer time with God. Once our badness is fully consumed, through the restorative practice of prayer, God returns goodness to us in the form of His forgiveness. All of us are free to confess and surrender our weaknesses, bad choices, and our lousy attitudes to God. He alone has the supernatural power to transform our messes into His heavenly masterpieces.[23] We are able to enjoy this privilege because the Bible tells us God gave his Son, Jesus, up unto death as payment for all of our sins:

> For God so loved the world that he gave his one and only Son, that whoever believes in him shall not perish but have eternal life.[24]

We can call upon Jesus' sacrifice whenever we are guilty of inappropriate or self-destructive thoughts, desires, or actions. We should claim God's merciful and unmerited favor by praising Jesus from our lips. We should frequently pray, "Thank you, Jesus Christ, that you paid the price for my sin and that my transgression is already forgotten by God. Thank you for forgiveness." The basic idea is that we should use our failures as reasons to run *towards* God in prayer, rather than as reasons to *run away* from Him in a useless attempt to hide and deny our imperfections.

Perhaps you are thinking, "Hey, *wait a minute*, I have done nothing wrong… I am a victim. Others have hurt me in the past." Why should a victim seek forgiveness from God? The answer is that God does not want us living with a victim's attitude. Romans 8:37 says Christians are "more than conquerors." Yet, if we allow negative thoughts (i.e., anger, resentment, fear, addictive urges, sadness, poor attitude, etc.) to fill our minds and overwhelm us, then we are not demonstrating a proper faith in God. That is the problem. We are not living life correctly if we let our past hurts rule over us. God should rule over us. People should seek aggressive healing and transformation of their bad past experiences; such toxic life narratives can be reshaped into better futures by seeking prayerful forgiveness.

The Counselor gleefully emphasized the irony of how the treacherous Gibeonites became the Israelites' slaves. The Gibeonites were ultimately required to carry ceremonial water to the Jewish Tabernacle. This labor of water-bearing was essential in its importance to the Jewish priests who could not enter the Tabernacle without first washing with the water. Given that this holy, cleansing water was an integral part of the Jewish ritual for worship, it is delightful and pleasing that this crucial component of godly worship was made available to the Jewish priests by the agents of Satan—the Gibeonites.

The Counselor then paused for a moment, and asked me, "Are you beginning to see how all of this works?" He went on to talk about how the Bible, in the book of Romans 8:28 (NIV), says that, "We know that in all things God works together with those who love him to bring about what is good—with those who have been called according to his purpose." With God's help, you can leverage the bad experiences of your life and use them as building blocks to shape a better future. The biblical foundation for the Joshua Protocol is built upon the idea that social and environmental conditioning and spiritual warfare are all real things that impact people's lives. But God is stronger than any evil, and we can benefit from God's power to thwart negative forces that attack us in this world. By worshipping God consistently and correctly, it is possible for the Lord to transform any evil and to simultaneously bring us closer to Him. When you choose to fashion a more intimate relationship with the creator of the universe, you will help yourself secure a better life with greater happiness and inner peace.

Seek Fellowship

Secondly, the Counselor explained how God's favor and mercy allow us to stand in amazing *fellowship* with Him. Such close

Stop Resisting Your Sins!

friendship comes as if we were blameless of any mistakes or wrongdoing in our lives. Of course, we are not in right standing with God based upon our own puny and imperfect efforts, but only through God's power can we be made whole and restored in His eyes. Satan hates it when we abide in, or spend time in companionship with God. After being murdered, Jesus conquered death by rising from the dead. He later ascended to heaven and sent us a Comforter and Helper in the form of the Holy Spirit.[25] This Holy Spirit is always available to us, but the devil wants us to try and face the turmoil of the world alone. If we separate ourselves from God, then we become vulnerable to Satan's tactics and risk our own destruction. But if we enjoy regular and close fellowship with the Lord, we can experience much greater peace and happiness. Attaining both godly forgiveness and fellowship are basic goals for those who use the Joshua Protocol.

Seek Discipline

Thirdly, the Counselor said that once we are done praying to God, we must finally leave the comfort that comes through prayerful relationship, and fully re-enter the physical world with all its troubles. But we do so knowing that we have undergone a spiritual change and have had our minds refreshed and restored. As we leave our prayer time, we can thank God for His "loving discipline"; the discipline that comes through God's perfect cleansing. The term *discipline* gives some people problems, as it often carries a lot of bad implications along with it. Most people associate the word *discipline* with the word *punishment*. But, for those who accept the Christian philosophy and actively live the Christian lifestyle, there is no penalty associated with godly discipline. This is because Jesus Christ died to pay the price for our mistakes. In 1 John 4:18, the Bible tells us that there is no punishment for those who embrace Christianity, as Jesus already suffered the punishment for us.[26] Two thousand years ago, Jesus accepted all the penalty we deserve today when he was killed on behalf of humanity. For this reason, the word *discipline* takes on a significantly different meaning for Christians.

Think of what is left over if you remove the idea of *punishment* from the word *discipline*. Absent any penalty, sanction, or hurtful consequence, what remains is the notion of God being our teacher and showing us the proper way to live. Discipline without punishment leaves us with a godly "coach," or God as our "tutor" or "mentor." Maybe you can think of godly discipline as like having a personal trainer at a gym or health club. But instead of body sculpting, God helps us learn how to sculpt our minds to achieve optimal mental health and joy. The point is the godly form of discipline—without any penalty or punishment—is wonderful. Godly discipline is a manifestation of God's grace and mercy. We should hungrily seek after it, and count it all as a blessing. It is a gift.

In an earlier section, I shared the biblical story of how the Gibeonite nation tricked Joshua and the Jewish people into accepting a peace treaty that went against the will of God. I explained how the Israelites eventually gained the upper hand by forcing the Gibeonites to serve as slaves who supported the Jewish process for God worship. The Counselor told me the Joshua Protocol method for prayer "carries the water and the wood" for us today, in much of the same way the Gibeonites did for the Israelite people, long ago. In other words, now we can be made whole and healthy and defeat evil through prayer. Evil and sin can be erased, and restoration may be attained by using the bad experiences of life to produce a good (or at least, better) future outcome. God has the transformative power to glean and sift goodness out of badness.

The conceptual breakthrough of the Joshua Protocol comes from understanding how all of our past efforts to resist sin have been thwarted by our humanity and our imperfections. But now, instead of fighting a constantly losing battle that depends on *our* limited willpower to resist sin, we can instead take the path of least effort and allow God to use his infinite power to transform our negativity into something better. Here is the bottom line: Stop resisting sin; instead, start transforming it. Use the unwanted habits and bad behaviors in your life as the basis for supercharging your spiritual relationship with God. Leverage your sins as catalysts to get yourself into a right relationship with the Lord, and then invoke godly spirituality to shape a better future life for yourself.

Thank Messages

The Counselor talked more about how best to pray. He said I should attempt to structure my prayers in the form of what he called "thank messages." He then offered another demonstration, whereby he verbally acted as someone waging an internal war against inappropriate thoughts, feelings, or actions. The Counselor advised me that when I feel full of shame or regret, due to my negative thoughts or behaviors, I should respond by saying something like the following:

> Lord, I am reminded of how thankful I should be towards you for cleansing me of my sins. Oh thank you, my Higher Power, my Heavenly Father, my God, for your forgiveness. *Thank you* for sending me a Savior named Jesus.

It is possible for people to come under attack by unseen spiritual forces. For some, it may sound farfetched, but the devil and his demonic spirits can try and plant toxic thoughts to take root in a person's brain. When such negative thoughts appear, it is important to respond immediately with prayer. The Counselor suggested I should consider praying something along the lines of:

> Oh God, Satan is insisting on putting this junk into my head. It only serves to remind me of my

constant fellowship with you, Lord. Your Holy Spirit is always with me and in me. I am never alone. Your holy presence indwells my body and mind. I feel a sense of great and peaceful comfort knowing that you are always right here with me. *Thank you* for investing your time and for staying close, wherever I go.

I, myself, have experienced periods when the devil has tried to corrupt my thought life. During such times, I was told that I should ponder about God's perfect discipline and how it benefits me. Here is an example:

Oh God, *thank you* for your loving discipline. You are such a gentleman that your perfect cleansing and grace hardly feel like "discipline" at all. I count it all as a blessing. There is no punishment for me. Christ accepted the penalty I deserve when he sacrificed his life on my behalf. *Thank you*, Lord, for loving me so much. I need to get back to my regular life activities now. But please be with me always.

Much in the same way as the Israelites turned the Gibeonites into their slaves, so can you and I turn the devil's evil intent to our advantage. We can transform harmful imagery and destructive thoughts into positive thank messages within the mind. Use the Lord's forgiveness, fellowship, and His loving discipline as heavenly weapons to wage your own successful spiritual warfare. You can change Satan's evil intent into positive prayer time spent with God. The Bible teaches we should not be overcome by evil, but overcome evil with good.[27]

Review of Counseling Session 2

1. The Counselor uses the biblical story found in chapter 9 of the book of Joshua to illustrate his essential point. Even our worst life experiences or choices can be made better, by calling upon the love and limitless power of God to provide transformation and restoration in our areas of hurt.
2. People can build character and grow their personal relationship with God by consistently seeking Him during times of trouble, and especially after they have made poor life choices and behaved unwisely.
3. God loves you, and He is pleased to extend His *forgiveness* to you, if you accept it.
4. God loves you, and He is eager for you to choose to engage in close *fellowship* with Him.
5. God loves you, and He is willing to bestow upon you His own unique brand of spiritual *discipline*. Godly discipline comes without condemnation, shame, or punishment. It is a huge blessing for a person to receive correction from the creator of the universe.
6. Thankfulness to God should be an integral part of a person's prayer life. Despite the hardships people face, if a person is honest, they can likely find something for which they may thank God.

Counseling Session 3
Key Concepts Explained

At the start of my third therapy session, the Counselor talked about how the secular healthcare community had begun to evolve its view of the human brain, starting back in the 1980s. He said, "There is something intangible about the human mind" and with the way people enjoy free will. He went on to say how, in the twentieth century, researchers discovered we can operate outside of the training and conditioning of our brains. Today, of course, we have a full-blown belief in the existence of higher consciousness. Moreover, most practitioners in the healthcare industry now believe that a person can alter their thinking and habits, by using the concept of neuroplasticity, or as I like to call it, brain change.

You can change your brain and grow your mind by using independent thought and conscious effort. If you do not exercise this ability to define yourself and to clearly establish your convictions and values, then you become a product of your environment and will be shaped by your life experiences. You will become like a piece of driftwood that is haphazardly tossed about in the ocean by the ferocious sea currents. The world and society will define who you are and will shape you as an individual. You will have turned control of your life over to fate.

Mindfulness

The Counselor introduced me to the work of psychiatrist, Jeffrey M. Schwartz, who wrote a bestselling book, *You Are Not Your Brain*. In his book, Dr. Schwartz explains the concept of *mindfulness* and underscores its importance for reprogramming the brain. Dr. Schwartz says that "mindfulness is awareness." He then goes on to say that mindfulness is "being fully knowledgeable that something is happening right now, in this very moment."[28] Dr. Schwartz suggests that when we become fully aware of the emergence of dysfunctional or damaging thoughts from our lower brains (he calls these thoughts "deceptive brain messages") then we are better positioned to defend our thinking by replacing negative thoughts with more positive ones.

If you consistently work to eliminate your negative attitudes and behaviors, and substitute positive thoughts to replace negative ones, then over time there will be physical changes that appear within the structure of your brain. The Counselor told me about how these physical changes happen in the neural pathways, and how brain circuitry can be refashioned. Earlier, we presented a simplified, two-part model of the human brain and discussed how our higher consciousness and our thoughts produce physical brain changes. By changing the circuitry of the brain, we can alter brain structure, and either reinforce or eradicate bad habits, unreasonable anxieties, or emotional dysfunctions. By exercising conscious decision-making, we can choose to have the kinds of brains we want, either positive or negative. Many clinicians within the healthcare community now believe that negative emotional thought patterns can be successfully defeated without the use of drugs. Good changes (even so-called "cures") may be realized in as little as one to two years.

The Counselor told me that chemical addictions to such things as drugs or alcohol can be harder to transform than behavioral or emotional problems, as the chemicals root better in the lower part of the human brain. This lower brain supports basic survival functions and is very animalistic. All of our experiences in life must pass through the lower brain first. It is within the lower brain that a quick determination is made to decide whether an immediate threat to life is present. The problem is that sometimes people get "stuck" in this portion of the brain, and certain stimuli never make it to the upper brain where the information can be properly evaluated by the mind. Upper brain functionality allows the mind to transcend the limitations of the instinctive lower brain. The upper brain and higher consciousness provide us with thinking and measured responses to the external stimuli we encounter in life.

It is essential to understand the difference between our instincts (quick reflexes) and our thoughts (carefully-weighed judgments). We can change who we are by understanding and modifying how we think. The practices of the military offer an excellent example of how people can be trained to override their lower, primal instincts. The military teaches soldiers to suppress their primal concerns for safety and survival, and to follow orders that could lead to great injury or death. Of course, in the developed world of today, most people do not live in a daily life-or-death struggle for existence. But in previous centuries, our ancestors lived dismal lives whereby they routinely depended upon their lower primal instincts to stave-off disaster and death. In ancient times, there was very little opportunity to engage in reflective higher-brain thinking. Now, however, most of us enjoy a relatively safe and calm existence. Today, the rule of law, combined with social safety nets and political and governmental service infrastructures, all afford us the luxury of moving beyond our primal instincts and thoughts. Today, we have the freedom, safety, spare time, and the opportunity to really stop and "think," using our higher-brain functionality.

At this point, the Counselor paused for a moment. His tone of voice suddenly changed, and he became quieter and more somber.

He continued to say that, unfortunately, the contemporary world seems to be squandering this opportunity for thoughtful and meaningful introspection. Instead, we seem to be devoting our spare time to idle pursuits such as video games, social media, sports entertainment, and the incessant quest for transient pleasure. We live in an amazing era that provides us the chance to transform ourselves, grow the mind, exercise free will, and supplant and transcend instinctual and survival modes. Theoretically, we should be able to achieve higher levels of enlightenment regarding the things of life that really matter. We should be building greater strength of character and acquiring wisdom that will allow us to achieve a mature form of happiness. We should be enjoying unparalleled contentment and peace and joy in our earthly existence. But the current reality seems to be just the opposite. In our world today, we appear to be losing ground. It looks like we are less able to deal with life stressors, than were our ancestors.

Without betraying any confidentiality, the Counselor proceeded to relate some of the general patterns he has observed in his client practice. For example, he told me about how some of his other therapy clients regularly suffer full-blown panic attacks when they do not excel on Wall Street, or when they fail to rapidly advance in their career or greed ambitions. He explained how such emotional reactions mimic the way our ancestors, of two hundred years ago, experienced the death of a spouse or a child. He concluded by saying we are losing our ability to cope with life. He argued that people in today's society are becoming weaker, precisely at a time when they should be getting stronger. Many individuals are losing their perspective and are regressing; they are becoming lesser people trapped within a devolving culture.

The Counselor went on to discuss how psychiatrists nowadays are doing important work in the field of psychology to support the notion of mind over brain. He continued by saying the brain is like a lump of clay, and it can be reshaped and cured of maladies by using "thought tools." These thought tools can redirect us and lead to changes in our thinking and behavior. For example, Obsessive-Compulsive Disorder (OCD) can be significantly improved in two months, according to Dr. Jeffrey M. Schwartz, whose work we referenced earlier.[29] Moreover, in Dr. Schwartz's book, he offers a four-step system for self-directed brain change, or neuroplasticity. Briefly, his four-step approach may be summarized as follows:

- *Relabel* to properly identify what is going on with your negative behaviors. (Tell yourself: "It's not me, it's my OCD. It's a medical condition causing these thoughts.")
- *Reattribute* is a reminder of the fact that your worry is connected to a bio-chemical medical condition. ("It's not me that is feeling worried, but it's my OCD that is making me feel like I'm worried.") Your identity must not get tied to the negative thoughts and behaviors.
- *Refocus* action onto some other more constructive behavior. This refocusing effort activates new brain circuitry and changes brain energy usage. The idea is to over-ride negative urges by engaging in other, more positive activities.
- *Revalue* allows the refocus step to happen more easily. This revalue process will take place automatically when you do the first three steps. The value of the compulsive sensation changes over time. It becomes less intense, as new brain circuitry is developed over several months.

Furthermore, Dr. Schwartz's "*Fifteen-Minute Rule*" says that if you can avoid having a specific negative thought or doing a negative behavior for fifteen-minutes (while substituting other, more positive activities) you will often find that you can resist doing the negative thing, altogether. Also, this fifteen-minute avoidance technique will jumpstart the building of new brain circuitry.

The Counselor went on to describe the work of another

brilliant physician and author, David D. Burns, MD, who wrote a bestselling book entitled, *Feeling Good*.[30] I was told that Dr. Burns encourages other psychiatrists to use thought tools as an alternative to medication for helping patients. He aims to give patients the chance to develop their upper brains and minds. Negative thinking can be changed into something more positive using the thought tool approach. The physical brain is an appliance that can be upgraded and grown. Drugs used in dealing with emotional problems only neutralize a person's ability to feel the problems; drugs do not help us to grow through challenges and have victory over them. But the use of thought tools can serve as a form of valuable mental "calisthenics" for strengthening our higher consciousness. The improved emotional state achieved with thought tools is real and positive; thought tools offer genuine hope for a better and healthier future.

> *Author's Note:* *I took the time here to briefly mention the work of Drs. Schwartz and Burns, to show how current practices used in the mental health field are compatible with the Joshua Protocol. Using an "It's not me" thought tool, and employing a concept like "refocus," are both very similar to the approach advocated by the Counselor.*

The Bodyguard

The Counselor went on to introduce a new subject for discussion. He started telling me about how people who fully embrace the Christian lifestyle enjoy a special type of supernatural protection. At first, I did not understand what he meant when he began talking about "the Bodyguard." But, this concept became a recurring theme during our discussions, and in the fullness of time, I started to piece his comments together. Ultimately, everything made better sense once I looked up the Scriptures he gave me, and found the following biblical passages that illustrate how God intervenes when His people need protection:

> But when they arrest you, do not worry about what to say or how to say it. At that time you will be given what to say, for it will not be you speaking, but the Spirit of your *Father* speaking through you.[31] (italics added)

And,

> Whenever you are arrested and brought to trial, do not worry beforehand about what to say. Just say whatever is given you at the time, for it is not you speaking, but the *Holy Spirit*.[32] (italics added)

In the spiritual sense, both Matthew and Mark list God, in the persons of the Father and of the Holy Spirit, as serving in the role of our "Bodyguard." God the Father sends angels and uses His power to protect us in the fight of good against evil. Additionally, the Holy Spirit lives and rules within everyone who chooses the Christian lifestyle. The Holy Spirit provides the children of God with a strong second layer of spiritual protection. Of course, I do not think the Bodyguard is a promise that we will never encounter harm. Instead, I think it is an assurance that worldly harm will not destroy us, spiritually. Paul writes:

> And God is faithful; he will not let you be tempted beyond what you can bear. But when you are tempted, he will also provide a way out so that you can endure it.[33]

The Counselor told me that each of us can also participate in the process of our self-protection, and help serve as our own bodyguard. We do so by creating, within the mind, functions and an awareness that allow us to discern good from evil. We must then develop and use the upper-brain neuroplastic circuitry needed to choose to do what we know is good. It can take people decades to achieve this sort of spiritual and mental conditioning. But it is this kind of character development that causes healthy individuals to avoid, and be repelled by, the corruption found in our broken world.

Hebrews 5:14 says only mature people, "by constant use," can discern good from evil. This means by experience and practice we train ourselves to habitually hold fast to what is good and to be repelled by what is bad. As we learn what God views as good and bad, we develop a defense system over time. We begin to differentiate between our upper-brain self and our lower-brain non-self. We can then attack, weaken, or even destroy our negative thoughts. The Counselor told me the dominance of mind over brain is called the "mind of Christ" within the context of the Bible. For example, 1 Corinthians 2:16 uses the phrase "mind of Christ" to describe a sharp intellect that helps us create opposition to negative thoughts. The Counselor went on to give me some additional background and examples on this subject. But for ease of understanding during my counseling sessions, the Counselor personified all the complex mental health scholarship and the available theological thinking on this topic and simplified it down to the term he uses—the Bodyguard.

Thoughts on Spiritual Purification

Our discussion then shifted slightly, as the Counselor addressed for me the idea of how to cleanse negative thoughts from the brain. He pointed to Galatians 2:20 that says Christ lives in us. The Counselor told me that we will not fully understand this Scriptural passage until we die and pass on to heaven where there will be clarity. However, he did go on to say that in this world, our lower brains house a mixture of conditioned responses that we acquire from our environment. Some of our societal conditioning is dysfunctional and not at all helpful or good for us. Nonetheless, it exists as programming buried deeply within our lower, primal, emotional brains. We subsequently do our best to process all the information, and we struggle to cope and to make sense of it using our higher intellect. Of course, Christians have the added advantage of being able to seek the help of the Holy Spirit and to use the teachings and biblical examples of Jesus Christ. By reaching into the supernatural sphere, Christians are better able to scrutinize and evaluate all of the surrounding environmental negativity. Ultimately, people must fight against all that is unhealthy in the brain, and for Christians, it is God "living in us" who defines what is legitimate versus what is damaging thought.[34]

The Counselor repeated that spiritual perfection comes to us in stages. It is a lengthy developmental process that begins during our life here on earth and extends into the afterlife. The apostle Paul talked about how, after we die, we will be brought to a certain level of perfection.[35] Then later, there will be introduced a new heaven and new earth, at which point even the knowledge of sin will be washed away—a new creation will be unveiled.[36] At that time, we will be brought to yet a higher level of perfection. It will be at that point in our spiritual development that a bodyguard will no longer be needed. Isaiah 11:6 talks about how the ferocious lion will make peace with the yearling calf and the lamb. No more evil will exist. We will have achieved true heaven.

Healthy Sex: One Love Relationship

The Counselor moved on with my therapy. He talked about how one powerful addiction, the addiction to inappropriate sexual behavior, can be successfully transformed by using the Joshua Protocol. Whether it is an addiction to pornography, adultery, fornication, prostitution, or other more deviant forms of behavior involving human sexuality, he explained about the need to correctly fashion the neural pathways of the brain to have a healthier view of sex. Since he was talking to me during a therapy session, he couched everything he said into male terms. But the concepts presented in the following lesson are illustrative for everyone.

The Counselor explained about the need to avoid false sexual images or fantasies. The Scriptural support he cited came out of Proverbs 5:15-20 (NIV):

> Drink water from your own cistern,
> running water from your own well.
> Should your springs overflow in the streets,
> your streams of water in the public squares?
> Let them be yours alone,
> never to be shared with strangers.
> May your fountain be blessed,
> and may you rejoice in the wife of your youth.
> A loving doe, a graceful deer—
> may her breasts satisfy you always,
> may you ever be intoxicated with her love.
> Why, my son, be intoxicated with another man's wife?
> Why embrace the bosom of a wayward woman?

The point of the above passage is to encourage the practice of marriage, with a focus on a spouse, to create an exclusive love relationship in your mind. Doing so breaks any dependency on other mental images, such as pornography or unhealthy daydreams. The male brain is unique in how it separates the object from the act. Men who are in a marriage relationship can engage in sexual fantasy and masturbation as a form of self-medication to ease the stresses and pressures of life. The man engages in this self-medication with no intent of harming his relationship with his spouse. But, from a female perspective, such behavior is harmful as women have an increased sensitivity in this area. The wife is made to feel unworthy and unloved when her husband turns to other images or thoughts to achieve sexual release.

The Counselor instructed me that God is both male and female, and to understand God, we must recognize how both genders operate. Men especially should consider how women, in many ways, represent the best of humanity. The Bible tells us how the woman came from the rib of a man; the rib rests over the heart and symbolizes the love, emotions, and feelings of God. God's feminine side needs to be better understood, and the Counselor emphasized that a husband can better understand the Lord when the husband establishes a closer emotional relationship with his wife. During his time on earth, the wife is her husband's bridge to reaching the fullest possible understanding of God. Men will never know more than biblical doctrine about God unless they make an effort to learn to love women properly. Comprehending "religious doctrine" is not the end point for knowing the Lord; women reflect and help men to better understand the fullness of God's emotions, relational senses, and feelings. The male and female brains are very different. Men need to grasp not only how males operate, but also how women behave. Husbands can better understand women by directing their exclusive love towards their wives.

Use Discipline to Shape Sexuality

We have already talked about the subject of discipline, as part of our explanation of the Joshua Protocol. But within the context of sex, discipline is what helps guide a person from having a sick thought life to a healthier one. Discipline prompts positive changes. But remember we said earlier how there is no punishment in the process of receiving godly discipline. Yet we expect punishment when we have wrong sexual thoughts or act out in ways that are inappropriate. If we ever feel pummeled with shame, guilt, or regret, we must understand such sentiments come from the belief that we should be forced to pay and suffer for our fallen sexuality. But the Bible tells a different story. For example, the New Testament teaches:

It is for freedom that Christ has set us free. Stand firm, then, and do not let yourselves be burdened again by a yoke of slavery.[37]

The Lord is pleased when we try to become healthier in both mind and brain. Whether we are struggling to improve our sexual identities, or are seeking to improve in other areas, God wants progress, not instant perfection. As we have said, punishment has already gone to the cross in the form of Christ who died for the sins of humanity.[38] Jesus has already died, and his sacrifice is payment in full for all our mistakes. It is finished.[39] Moreover, if you adopt a lifestyle similar to that of Christ, it will bring power to you so that you can change your brain by reprogramming it, thereby removing the negativity and obsessiveness that has robbed you of real joy in life.

The Counselor went on to say, like the Old Testament Jews with the Gibeonites, we have also been deceived by our contemporary world to engage in unhealthy practices. As a result, we now find ourselves with a bunch of toxic trash in our thinking. The answer is to reduce the power of such thoughts by making their negativity our slave. Make the negativity "carry our wood" (our sin) to the altar of Godly worship, and then burn the sin to cinders through prayer. We can stop the momentum of Satan— stop him at the place of the cross using the ways of God to burn-up the sin so we can be free, and live better lives.

Being thankful is also essential. If we practice thankfulness, we will mature in life. Our aim should be to make our gratitude outgrow our areas of failure and our bad habits. If we feel any pain at all from God, it is not aimed at us, but instead at the cancer-like, tumor-like sin buried within us. The Counselor spoke of the "externalization" of the sin, and understanding "It's not me." Our goal must be to lower the frequency, intensity, and duration of negative acts and wrong thoughts. It is a developmental process that takes time and constant practice. We begin by consistently mocking the enemy inside of us. Whether the ultimate source of our problem comes from the primal brain, or from something supernatural and evil that attacks from outside of ourselves, we must unmask the enemy and clearly identify it as something *separate* from us.

A helpful technique for separating our conscious mind from any toxic thinking involves our ability to learn to create a psychological "space" between the upper brain, and any damaging thoughts we may experience in the primal, lower brain. Dr. Caroline Leaf is a Christian communication pathologist and audiologist who explains in her book, Switch On Your Brain, how we should mindfully see ourselves as if we were, "An outsider looking in through a window."[40] This is to say, whenever we need to combat a compulsive desire or a negative thought, we should attempt to pause for a few seconds and figuratively "step out of our own heads." By mentally positioning ourselves outside of a stressful or difficult circumstance, we create a small degree of separation from our primal brains. By providing this small gap, we can then better empower our upper-brains to take charge of the situation. The result is that we can use the power of our minds to increase our chances of making healthier choices in the moment.

Ultimately, the Counselor said we should strive to become an extension of Jesus Christ in our thinking. There exists both objective good and evil. As living creatures in a fallen world, we require both spiritual and physical healing. The Counselor said that, "Washing with the water of the Word is a form of holy labor."[41] We can begin this labor by taking the time and making an effort to better understand the valuable lessons taught through the content found in the Bible. The learning process is much like what we have already seen in the book of Joshua with our discussion of the Gibeonites. Such holy labor requires a life-long commitment to scriptural study. The task may seem overwhelming, but the longest voyage begins with a small first step. As we learn, grow, and achieve greater health and happiness, we will start to enjoy and savor the journey.

Eric Roderiques

Scriptures for Defining Godly Discipline

As we have said, people often associate the word *discipline* with the word *punishment*. But God's definition of discipline is different. For those who have embraced the Christian lifestyle, there is no punishment when dealing with God. The following four scriptures from the Bible help illustrate this idea:

God is love.[42]

There is no fear in love. But perfect love drives out fear, because fear has to do with punishment. The one who fears is not made perfect in love.[43]

But if we confess our sins to him, he can be depended on to forgive us and to cleanse us from every wrong. And it is perfectly proper for God to do this for us because Christ died to wash away our sins.[44]

There is therefore now no condemnation for those who are in Christ Jesus.[45]

Without the fear of punishment, the godly brand of discipline is unlike that which is commonly doled out by our society and culture. God's perfect discipline takes the form of gently teaching, coaching, mentoring, and training us in His healthier ways of living. God wants to make a personal investment in each of us, and all He requires is our willingness to remain under His loving tutelage and care.

If we are open to the idea of allowing God to enter our lives, His mercy will replace the old psychological conditioning, mental and emotional hangups, the primal instincts, and bad habits that are common in the lower brain. Receiving God's mercy is the ultimate way to fix the damage from our past bad experiences. Understand that the higher mind and consciousness, which by nature starts out as weak, can be trained to stand-up against the powerful programming of the lower brain. With diligent practice, each of us can change our thinking, as well as the physical structure of our brains. We can subsequently change the patterns of our lives and choose to live much as Christ did. But first we need to stop being victims of biology and of our past life experiences, and instead, fight for the future existence we really want. We must use methodologies and modern concepts, like neuroplasticity, to change the physical wiring of the brain. We can reject the life that is being forced upon us by our environment and past life history. In its place, we can choose to pursue the life described in the Scriptures and achieve an inner peace that surpasses understanding.[46] The point of many of Jesus' teachings is that if we do not decide to follow him, we will fatalistically fall victim to our toxic environment and to negative societal influences and pressures.

Sharing in God's Reality

The term *cognition* refers to thinking. The term *affect* refers to feeling and emotion. The process of actively changing our negative thinking is known as *cognitive behavioral therapy* (CBT). But improved cognition is not enough. The Counselor advocates the addition of a separate affective component to our therapy process. This is to say, it is possible to enhance our healing outcome significantly by adding an additional *spiritual* dimension to our therapy.

In this sense, *affective therapy* seeks to thoroughly understand, not just God's thoughts, convictions, and beliefs as they would relate to cognitive therapy—but also the rich emotional life of God. In the context of affective therapeutic approaches, the definition of being "in reality" must include being in harmony with God's thought and affect (i.e., being in harmony with God's mind, feelings, and values). We must try to incorporate the Lord's way of doing things into our lives. This is because only God enjoys an understanding of absolute reality and truth.

To grasp absolute reality, a person would need to be all-knowing. As humans, we require God's assistance to glimpse at the truth of life and the universe.[47] On our own, we can only guess about what life is supposed to be. Moreover, without God, we cannot defend ourselves against evil, nor can we embrace objective good since we have an inadequate frame of reference to know absolute good. But all of this discussion raises the question of how a person can come to know the feelings and values of God? The answer is that such knowledge comes from studying and understanding the teachings of the Bible. C.S. Lewis, in *Mere Christianity*, compared the study of Christian theology to the use of a road map. Lewis said, "If you want to go anywhere, the map is absolutely necessary." The Bible is the ultimate road map for Christians. It directs us to a closer relationship and better understanding of God.

The Counselor challenged me to think of the human brain as being like a diseased kidney that requires the help of a dialysis machine. But the dialysis machine we must use to clean the brain involves our turning away from our bad habits and looking towards God to learn how to live properly. We should not emphasize our dysfunction, but emphasize our dependence upon the Lord. The longer you think about your sin, the more powerful you make those negative feelings that are associated with it. It is like forever staying in Good Friday, the day when Jesus was murdered, and never moving on to celebrate Easter Sunday—the day when Christ arose from the dead and forever conquered evil. We must mentally and emotionally "die" to the negative thoughts and beliefs that others and our environment have placed into us. The best way to vanquish evil in ourselves is to build-up the good within us until it overpowers the bad. The apostle Paul tells us to overcome evil with good.[48] We should make a sustained effort to press through the negativity in our lives. We must struggle to turn our back on sin and our face toward God.

Review of Counseling Session 3

1. *Mindfulness,* or self-awareness in the moment, helps you to become more self-directed and stay in better control of your life. The alternative is to allow external forces to determine and direct your activities and purpose. When you lack mindfulness, the expectations and pressures imposed by people, society, culture, or your personal circumstances can sweep you away and take control of your life and destiny.
2. *The Bodyguard* is a type of spiritual protection that is available to everyone who freely embraces the Christian lifestyle. It derives mainly from God's limitless spiritual power, but you can also help protect yourself once you grow in character and develop your own internal ability to discern good from evil, and to resist evil.
3. Healthy sexuality and successful human relationships depend upon a commitment to marriage and one exclusive love relationship with a spouse.
4. Embracing godly discipline to promote character development is key to shaping healthy sexuality. It is important to note that God's brand of discipline is absent any punishment. God loves you and wants to teach you His approach to a better life.
5. Although He may not always approve of your choices and habits, the Lord is not angry with you. Instead, He hopes you will pursue a close personal relationship with Him. God is a gentleman. He does not force Himself upon His children but waits for us to approach Him.
6. According to C.S. Lewis, Christian theology is like a "road map" that can direct and guide you as you seek to build a better understanding of the ways and truth of God.

Counseling Session 4
A Deeper Understanding

To better comprehend God, you need to use the upper portion of your brain, where your mind and spirit are housed. Moreover, you must be able to think abstractly. The Counselor explained that God is neither "black and white" nor "right and wrong." God is complex and powerful. God sees a difference between the disease of sin and the person who is infected with the disease. Any corrective action that God launches is aimed at addressing our sin; it is not aimed at us. Unfortunately, our physiology (our flesh) gets in the way and we can, therefore, sometimes feel pain as God attacks the sin inside of us. We can wrongly think we are being "punished," or that the Lord is angry with us. In fact, Hebrews 12 says that God loves us and is using a process like that of a dialysis machine whereby we are being cleansed from the impurities of our experiences and societal inputs.[49] There is no punishment for us, as Christ suffered punishment in our place when he was crucified. For Christians, our debt has already been paid by Jesus. Our sins have been forgiven. God loves us as His children.

The additional good news is that, as you consistently use the Joshua Protocol approach of offering "thank you" messages to God, the prayers gradually create a virtuous cycle of improvement. Through your positive and determined efforts, the result will ultimately be one whereby your old habits, compulsions, obsessions, and rituals start to fade into insignificance. As you become more experienced at applying the prayer methodology suggested in this book, you will gradually develop a capacity to move past any residual addictive or destructive urges you experience. Therapist George N. Collins talks about how, once you become healthier, "You won't have as many addictive impulses to defend against. Those that do arise will be like fruit flies buzzing around your head—you can begin to easily shoo them away."[50] Moreover, if and when you occasionally slip and fall, you will be able to promptly shake-off any resulting shame, guilt, and regret, and rapidly resume a normal life that is productive and useful in its service to God and to others around you in society.

Some Failure is Normal

Excellence is not perfection.[51] Typically, when we have a behavioral lapse or a "break" in chastity, sobriety, or wise decision-making, the tendency is to then fall into a deep pit of shame, guilt, and regret. Such periods of emotional upset can last hours or even days after an incident. Satan exploits our feelings to render us worthless as a resource to God. God wants to include us in His good plan for this world. Remember that the Bible calls the devil the "accuser of the brethren," and he attacks when and where we are most vulnerable.[52] Often, the devil will emotionally confront us immediately after we have succumbed to temptation. Once you do something wrong or foolish, the devil starts to torment you in an effort to make your self-esteem crash.

Satan wants you to fall into a pit of depression so the Lord will not be able to use you to help advance God's agenda here on earth. But if you use the approach of the Joshua Protocol, you can respond differently whenever you make mistakes. By quickly admitting any sins to God, you can promptly receive forgiveness and be granted God's pardon. You can swiftly regain your emotional balance as you move forward; you can be instantly forgiven, restored, and rendered sinless by remembering the shed blood and sacrifice of

Christ. You will ultimately enjoy a triumph over your former bad habits, bad thinking, or harmful rituals. God can transform you into a new creature.[53] Furthermore, as you build your personal relationship with the Lord, you will experience progressively fewer ethical or moral failures in the time ahead.

But Satan will not give up easily. He will use any weapon he can to defeat you. Later in your journey, as you consistently apply the Joshua Protocol and become stronger, the devil will grow more desperate to hurt you. He might choose to delve deep into your life history and dredge up old and obscure memories of your past mistakes to use as weapons against you. For example, I recall the time when I was nearly a year into my recovery program, and was making serious forward strides and could see tremendous improvements in both my behavior and attitude. Then, one night as I lay in bed trying to go to sleep, I was unexpectedly attacked by a rogue thought that seemed to come out of nowhere.

The Story of Bobby

As I lay quietly in the dark of my bedroom, I suddenly remembered something I had done during my youth, some thirty years earlier. With the passage of the decades, the episode had faded from my remembrance. It had to do with my dealings involving a young neighbor boy whom I had encountered when I was a college freshman. I was around the age of eighteen, and this young neighbor child was no more than eight years old. I was still living at home with my parents, in the house in which I had grown up in California. The child, whom I will call Bobby, was a happy, freckled-faced red-haired boy. Bobby lived with his parents in the house across the street.

I recall that early each morning, I would ride my bicycle to the college campus. I remember always feeling stressed and hurried as I rushed off to school for my freshman classes. Young Bobby would rise early in the day, and would already be playing in his front yard when it was time for me to leave for school. Young Bobby knew my name and sought my friendship, in the way a young boy covets the friendship of an older male. Each morning I would race by Bobby's house atop my bicycle, and Bobby would greet me with a friendly *"Hi Eric!"* as I whizzed past him as he stood on the sidewalk in front of his house.

I remembered feeling annoyed by Bobby's attempts to connect with me and to build a relationship. I felt like I had no time and no need to interact with a child. After all, I was busy trying to adapt to my college experience and was transitioning into young adulthood. All that consumed me were thoughts of classes, school grades, and concerns about future success in the competitive academic world of a university. I was too stressed, and in fact, I felt it was somehow *beneath* me to engage with this young child; a child who had become a bother and an irksome distraction to me each morning. I decided that I would just ignore the boy's daily greetings and not even make eye contact as I sped past Bobby, on my way to school.

For weeks after that, each day, Bobby would repeat his friendly *"Hi Eric!"* greeting to me as I raced past him on my bicycle. And each day, I would respond with stony silence. For a time, I could hear an increased urgency from Bobby, when he would shout out more loudly *"Eric!!"* in a vain and increasingly desperate attempt to compel my attention and win my response and approval. I would sometimes steal a quick glance at Bobby as I rode swiftly by him on the street. I could see the bewilderment and sadness on his young face. After weeks of persistent effort, Bobby finally gave up. And subsequently, for weeks more, Bobby continued to observe me in complete silence as I passed by him each morning. I can only imagine the sense of confusion and rejection Bobby must have experienced. I devalued the youngster and must have made him feel unworthy as a person. I can only guess at the level of hurt I caused in him.

As I already mentioned, thirty years later, while lying patiently in a darkened bedroom waiting to go to sleep, Satan resurrected those old memories of my past encounters with Bobby. Like an avalanche of guilt, shame, and regret, the devil sought to devastate me emotionally with the remembrance of my callous insensitivity to a beautiful young child. As I lay in my bed, I endured several minutes of tormented emotional anguish. I replayed the story of Bobby in my mind, and tears began to roll uncontrollably down the sides of my face. But then something told me I was experiencing a spiritual attack. Why else would I suddenly think of something that took place a generation earlier? The whole emotional experience was surreal and inexplicable.

Unleashing the Power of Prayer

Once I realized what was happening, I immediately started using the Joshua Protocol prayer method. I understood that I was no longer the same person who had so thoughtlessly ignored the emotional needs of a young child. *It wasn't me* anymore. I then quickly prayed for and received God's *forgiveness* for my earlier wrong behavior. Moreover, I gave thanks for God's *fellowship* that had been so instrumental in my personal growth into adulthood, during all the years and decades after my encounter with Bobby. I also thanked the Lord for his perfect *discipline*, which came in the form of the tutoring and mentoring I had needed to change, grow, and become a better person. Lastly, I prayed for Bobby's welfare. I have no idea what eventually became of the youngster, who is now an adult. But I asked God to shield and protect Bobby and to restore him from any hurts or sadness that I may have foolishly caused when Bobby was a child. God is amazingly brilliant, limitlessly powerful, and infinitely creative. He can reshape the very fabric of time and space. Even prayers offered, a generation later, can prompt God to rewrite history and bring about present-day restoration, healing, and joy to those who had been hurt.[54]

Eric Roderiques

What Does Satan Want?

Why do people hurt other people? What is going on in the world today? Why is the devil waging a spiritual war against God and humanity? The answers lie in the biblical truth that Satan's future has already been decided by God. If we study the Bible, we can have a better understanding of the current world situation and the nature of the challenges people face. One scriptural passage says, "And the devil that deceived them was thrown into the lake of fire and brimstone, where the beast and the false prophet are also; and they will be tormented day and night forever and ever."[55]

In the end, Satan will be stopped and thoroughly punished. But misery loves company. Satan and his demons do not want to forever suffer alone in hell. They want humanity to suffer along with them. As you read these words, the devil is waging a war of frustration against God and against God's people. Satan knows that both he and his demonic followers are doomed. Therefore, the devil has adopted a kind of "scorched earth" policy whereby he is attempting to create maximum havoc within God's physical universe before the devil's final demise. Precisely because God so loves the world, and all of humanity within it, Satan has targeted people for special attack and attempted destruction.[56] The devil hopes to strike at God through God's beloved children—through you and me.

In his fantasy story, *The Screwtape Letters*, C.S. Lewis offers a chilling depiction of the devil's plan for humanity. By encouraging behaviors designed to corrupt the human soul, Satan intends to later claim ownership and control over the spirits of fallen people. C.S. Lewis imagines how Satan and his demons in hell aim to somehow spiritually "consume" their human victims—as if human souls were a kind of pleasing food or drink for the enemies of God. Lewis suggests this nightmare scenario would provide Satan and his demonic followers with some measure of comfort in the future once they, themselves, are sentenced by God to an eternity of suffering in hell. In Lewis' book, a minor demon is sternly warned by a master demon:

> But do remember, if any present self-indulgence on your part leads to the ultimate loss of the [human] prey, you will be left eternally thirsting. If, on the other hand, by steady and cool-headed application you can finally secure his soul, he will then be yours forever—a brim-full living chalice of despair and horror and astonishment which you can raise to your lips as often as you please.

The source of the devil's hatred of humanity is one of jealousy. God's plan for His people is both good and awesome. God wants to anoint humanity with an exalted heavenly status that Satan, long ago, had tried to forcibly take for himself. The Bible explains Lucifer's original ambitions in the book of Isaiah 14:13-16 (NASB). The following excerpt is an eye-opening look at both a history and a future yet to come. It begins by telling of how an amazing and beautiful creation of God, a super-angel named Lucifer, long ago chose to rebel against heaven. The power and beauty that God had originally gifted to Lucifer became a source of sinful pride. As a result of his pride, Lucifer chose to shun goodness and to become evil. Moreover, he proceeded to recruit an angelic army to fight a war against God. Lucifer and his demonic followers wanted to displace God and take control of heaven and the universe, instead of the Lord. The Bible concisely tells the story of how the former arch-angel, who became known as Satan or the devil, failed in his attempt to conquer heaven and defeat God. Moreover, the very last part of the following Scripture hints at humanity's special place in heaven's plan. Godly men and women will one day look down at the devil, and Satan will appear puny and insignificant as he languishes forever amidst the torments of hell:

> But you [Lucifer] said in your heart,
> "I will ascend to heaven;
> I will raise my throne above the stars of God,
> And I will sit on the mount of assembly
> In the recesses of the north.
>
> I will ascend above the heights of the clouds;
> I will make myself like the Most High [God]."
>
> Nevertheless, you [Satan]
> will be thrust down to Sheol [hell],
> To the recesses of the pit.
>
> Those [godly humans] who see you [in the future]
> will gaze at you,
> They will ponder over you, *saying*,
> "Is this the man [Satan] who made the earth tremble,
> Who shook kingdoms[?]"

After the angelic rebellion in heaven had failed, God created a new race of beings known as *humanity*.[57] Humanity has been adopted by God into His own royal family. Romans 8:17 describes how humans are "heirs of God and joint heirs with Christ." Through the process of adoption, God plans to groom and prepare humanity to enter into God's family as a type of spiritual royalty that will one-day rule, along with God, in heaven.[58] The reason why Satan hates people so much is that God plans to voluntarily give to humanity the very things that Lucifer, and his fallen angels, had sought to take for themselves by force. Satan, therefore, despises people and seeks to destroy them. Satan despises *you*. He is willing to use any means available to defeat and keep you from benefiting from God's good plan for your future. Alcohol, drugs, anger, and inappropriate relationships are just some of the many weapons of warfare the devil will use to try and destroy you.

Stop Resisting Your Sins!

Unreasonable fear and anxiety are additional tools the devil can use to keep you off-balance, as Satan will try to use apprehension and worry to render your life both ineffective and miserable.

Conquering Baseless or Unreasonable Fear and Anxiety

The Counselor told me that we can use the approach of the Joshua Protocol to fight our negative thinking and the weak faith that often results from our poor attitudes and habits. Whenever we experience ripples of unwarranted fear sweeping over us, we should quickly move to transform such fear and anxiety into godly worship by taking the following action steps. Immediately think or say, "That's not me!" and understand that fear is often irrational. Dr. Rudolph Tanzi of Harvard Medical School talks about creating "a small gap" between you and your emotions.[59] In other words, try to observe yourself in the moment, and think, "This is just me feeling anxious."

Mentally step back and away from your emotions, and instead lean on the truth that is told in the Bible. We already mentioned Romans 8:28, the scriptural passage that assures us God has an overall plan for good. Ephesians 6 says that Christians have the whole "Armor of God" to protect them. Moreover, Romans 8:37 says that we are more than conquerors through God. Philippians 4:6 tells us not to worry about anything, but, pray about everything. Lastly, 1 Peter 5:9 (TLB) says to "Stand firm when Satan attacks. Trust the Lord." It is hard for many to comprehend and believe, but for Christian people, fear and anxiety are unnecessary responses to life's events and troubles. This is true because God has His followers spiritually protected. I am not saying the experiences of a Christian are always perfect and pain-free. But I am saying Christianity, as a lifestyle, helps a person to better cope with the challenges of this world.

Armed with the Bible's wisdom and encouragement regarding our ultimate safety, we can quickly give thanks to God for His *forgiveness* of our weak faith and wrong thinking. We can also thank God for His *fellowship* and protection against any fear that the world presents. We are never alone. Further, we should thank Him for perfect *discipline*—God's teaching, coaching, mentoring, and nurturing. All of God's discipline comes without punishment because Jesus took all the punishment on our behalf when he was martyred to atone for the sins of humanity. Christians can grow in their understanding that God's brand of discipline is a wonderful gift. Moreover, within the framework of our earlier discussion on neuroplasticity, we can appreciate how thankfulness grows health in the human brain, while negativity grows illness. The Holy Spirit responds favorably to our thank messages. When we complain about circumstances, we are in fact passing judgments about our situation and showing our lack of faith in God. Who are we to judge or criticize anything, or anyone? We are least qualified to be judging or criticizing God.

The Pain of Healing

Once you decide that you want to get better, be ready to experience some pain. There is an initial pain in healing when you start using the Joshua Protocol. Most people are familiar with what happens to an alcoholic or a drug addict who suddenly quits alcohol or other drugs. Addicts experience chemical withdrawal symptoms when their bodies are suddenly denied the addictive substances they crave. A similar experience of "withdrawal" happens when you begin applying the Joshua Protocol to your life and start to wean yourself from inappropriate habits, thoughts, attitudes, or unhealthy practices.

I remember sitting in the Counselor's office and complaining to him: "Hey, you didn't tell me that this Joshua Protocol involves *pain*. When I walk through a shopping center, I *enjoy* looking at those giant, racy lingerie sales displays in the store windows! And I *like* fantasizing about the lovely young female fashion models I see portrayed everywhere throughout the mass media." The bottom-line is that whether somebody is quitting recreational drug use, or is trying to break bad habits like gambling, alcohol, or porn, the subsequent denial of pleasure hurts. It is a real form of pain.

As I say, positive changes can sometimes be hurtful and unpleasant at the beginning. We can experience temporary pain, even when the change promises to make us happier later in life. It is the "later" part that causes us the trouble. We do not want to feel good later; we want to feel good right now. We are in a world full of people who desire instant gratification. But Paul, in Galatians 5:24 (NIV) said, "Those who belong to Christ Jesus have crucified the flesh with its passions and desires." Paul also talked about the idea of dying to self, and about how he emotionally and attitudinally had to "die daily" to sinful temptations.[60] Expect some short-term discomfort as you experience your early withdrawal symptoms. Joyce Meyer, Bible teacher and best-selling author of her book, *Battlefield of the Mind*, says the pain of addiction and bondage to sin lasts forever, while the pain of getting healthier eventually subsides. Short-term hurt is the price we must pay to achieve greater joy over the long-term. Joyce Meyer challenges you to choose your brand of pain wisely.

The Counselor assured me the pain of Good Friday will always result in a celebration of victory on Easter Sunday. He used the Good Friday versus Easter comparison often. Jesus suffered terribly on the cross, only to say, "Father, forgive them, for they know not what they do."[61] Although the experience of Good Friday was a physical and emotional horror for Jesus, he was, nonetheless, able to see beyond His own pain and anguish in the moment. Jesus had the mindfulness to see through the cross that would bring about His death, and glimpse the spiritual victory that lay just beyond. We, too, are called by God to develop a similar kind of divine vision. We must not become discouraged. Our pain and discomfort will become less as we get stronger and move closer to attaining freedom over our negative habits, thoughts, or harmful rituals.

The Counselor commented that it was Moses, from the Bible's Old Testament, who first shared a godly message of hope with the Israelite people. Moses became a role model who taught how God wanted people to live. Part of God's promise is that, "This commandment that I'm commanding you today isn't too much for you, it's not out of your reach."[62] Also, Isaiah 40:29-31 and Isaiah 41:10 have God promising to strengthen us during our times of trial. As I said above, once we choose the path to health and wellness, our capacity to resist temptations, obsessions, and addictions will begin to grow stronger. Moreover, the Joshua Protocol will help us to promptly cleanse and right ourselves, should we occasionally stumble.

Some people will read this section and think to themselves, "I'm not ready for this. I want what I want. I'm not ready to give up my lifestyle choices, and I'm certainly not interested in curbing my physical and emotional pleasures." In fact, the Counselor told me he has encountered individuals who were very active in the human sexuality movement; people who engage in sex orgies every weekend. Some of these people see no ethical issues associated with their lifestyle. These people are happy and content with their choices. The Counselor responds by saying that he, in turn, must maintain his professional distance and is obligated to respect the decisions of his clients and others who choose to embrace dangerous or unhealthy lifestyles. His view is like that of Jesus who accepted the choice of the rich young ruler who declined Jesus' offer of close fellowship.[63] The Counselor supports his clients as "free agents" who make decisions about the kind and quality of lives they seek to live.

But I think there is much good to be said about a lifestyle of moderation. I would argue self-control, in all aspects of life, is a worthwhile skill to practice and develop. The Bible advises us to exercise temperance in all things. 1 Peter 5:8 instructs us to be well-balanced and be on the alert, lest we are devoured by the challenges of life. Paul said he buffeted his body each day to keep it in check and under control.[64] As I mentioned earlier in this book, there are people detained in prison right now because they failed to curb their emotional impulses. If we choose to deny the need for self-discipline in our lives, we are opening the door to a host of dangerous possibilities for our future.

Perfect Sex: In the Garden of Eden

The Counselor returned to the subject of human sexuality. He described God as "ultimate beauty," and referenced the Old Testament's Song of Solomon, which is a biblical love poem. He said the Song of Solomon is highly symbolic and teaches us how we can personally experience God's love. <u>Our relationship with God impacts all of our other relationships, including that which we enjoy with a spouse.</u> The Counselor went on to say the beauty of God is greater than any earthly fantasy, and our friendship with our Lord is greater than the temporary pleasure that can be found in an illicit sexual affair, or any other inappropriate interpersonal associations. Our goal should be to want more out of life. But the correct path to "more" should be found in our close and growing relationship with God.[65]

As we take steps to become healthier, the beauty of God we experience in our lives will increase over time. But there is an everyday battle we must face. This battle involves the bending of the self-will. This is to say, if we want to have a good life here on earth, we need to control our thoughts and actions. Ideally, we should experience the love feast between God's spirit and our spirit as the main source of enjoyment in life. This love relationship with the Lord also affects our relationships with our spouse and everybody else with whom we come into contact. The more you love the wrong way, the more your sensory capabilities are damaged and ultimately atrophy. It is as if "your taste buds die," explained the Counselor. But, fortunately, our sensory "taste buds" can be revived and we can again learn to correctly enjoy all the pleasant, robust flavors of life.

Eric Roderiques

The Peach and the Candy Bar

Here is a quick mental exercise to illustrate the above point. Imagine that you are hungry. Very hungry. You have not eaten all day long. You finally get home, and on your kitchen table you see a fresh, ripe, whole peach. Without thinking, you voraciously begin to devour the lovely piece of fruit. It is succulent, sweet, and delicious. You ravenously enjoy every morsel of the food. But now, suppose the same story had happened differently. Instead of coming home to see a fresh piece of fruit, you arrive and find your favorite variety of candy bar sitting on your kitchen counter. You immediately tear open the factory packaging and quickly consume the sugary confection. Its smooth and creamy texture is luscious, and its flavor is scrumptious. Nevertheless, once the candy is gone, you are still hungry. But, at the opposite end of the kitchen counter you spot a fresh, ripe, whole peach. You promptly pick up the peach and take a big, juicy bite of it into your mouth. You begin to chew and instantly notice that the fruit tastes sour and bitter. You do not enjoy the taste of the ripened peach at all. What happened?

Your sense of taste was distorted. The man-made, factory produced, sugar and chemical laden candy bar dramatically altered your ability to appreciate normal food flavors in your mouth. Typically, your body can enjoy what nature presents as authentic food. But in the situation I described above, you allowed a processed, artificial, "junk food" experience of a candy bar to distort your body's sensory capabilities. Your sense of taste betrayed you, as it was no longer able to appreciate the healthy food that nature intended for your body to consume. This simple illustration shows what can happen to us in society.

Whether we partake of illegal narcotics, abuse alcohol, pervert sex, or engage in other unwholesome practices, we run the risk of losing our ability to feel and experience life correctly. Unhealthy pleasures skew our expectations of what life is all about and cause us to lose our perspective and our ability to enjoy the normal, good things of life. A reasonable and healthy lifestyle can be made to seem inadequate, even dull, as we covet culturally-encouraged but perverse and synthetic experiences that can sometimes become toxic and dangerous. To prevent this from happening, we must carefully and consistently refocus and moderate our emotions, thoughts, actions, and our lifestyle.

Regarding the subject of sex, society often offers extreme and twisted representations that serve only to confuse and frustrate us about what we should want from our sexuality. The Counselor said that both the challenge and the answer to this problem is to become a "lover of God." Sadly, many of us do not know how to think of love, except in erotic ways. This fact can damage our prayer life for a while, but we can eventually get past the problem as we grow spiritually. One day, it will be possible for us to experience pure and innocent love on a scale we could never have dreamt of before. There will be joy in the affective (emotional) part of us. We will have a fullness of life in both our spirit and in our privacy, but also in the openness of our relationships and in our outward behavioral life.

All this can be accomplished, in large measure, by invoking God's forgiveness, fellowship, and discipline, through the Joshua Protocol methodology. We must use what the Counselor called "gratuitous cleansing" in the form of constantly giving thanks to God and maintaining a close personal relationship with Him. We should strive to pray without ceasing and must be consciously aware of who we are in God's eyes.[66] When we are constantly refreshed, spiritually, we may subsequently enjoy the benefits of God's loving discipline, which makes us grow better and healthier. This is how we defeat our spiritual enemy, the devil, and win our personal victory.

At this point, I became frustrated with the Counselor. All his commentary on the topic of sex had seemed so flowery, perfumed, rhetorical, ethereal, and far too lofty for me. For example, I recall verbally lashing out when he referenced the Bible's Song of

Solomon: "That's just poetry!" I remarked with clear irritation. "I want to talk about *sex*. Okay, okay, I admit it. I messed-up my brain. Long ago, I polluted my head with a bunch of junk; all the stuff I saw and heard and did. I know now that it was all a lie. A perversion of God's intent. I get it. But now, I want to know what sex *should* be."

"Excellent question," the Counselor replied calmly and smoothly.

He then went on to explain his understanding of the truth. Based upon the sum total of his combined decades of scholarship and life experience, the Counselor proceeded to share with me some of his personal philosophy for comprehending the plans and ways of God. He started off by repeating that today's expectations for human sexuality are twisted, unreasonable, and false. From a Christian perspective, the question should be: *What kind of sex did Adam and Eve most likely enjoy in the Garden of Eden, before the Fall of Humanity and before sin was introduced to the world?* In other words, what does the term "innocent sex" mean?

For some people, the words "innocent" and "sex" sound like complete opposites, and combining these terms make for a laughable joke. But what did God most likely have in mind before sin appeared, and before sin perverted God's plan for healthy human sexuality? The Counselor said that to better understand the problem with sex, we should think of sex as being like a large mirror. Within this mirror is captured the reflection of God's perfect vision for human sexuality, and for life in general.[67] The Counselor went on to explain that sin "smashes" the mirror, creating a shattered array of thousands upon thousands of small prisms that distort the reality of godly sex and a godly life. Because of the damage inflicted by sin, it has become difficult for humanity to gain an accurate perspective on how to live, and we can easily be led astray into wrong directions when it comes to the behaviors we choose and the life choices we make.

Stop Resisting Your Sins!

Shattered World

Both individually, and together as a fallen culture, we are tortured as we try and make sense of the broken mirror pieces. We as individuals become fragmented whenever we enter into destructive acts or relationships. When it comes to the subject of sex, we often mistakenly seek to achieve the extreme erotic ideals of our twisted and sick society. As a result, our personal perceptions of God and our understanding of what is appropriate conduct, all become distorted. Only through reconciliation, maturation, regeneration, and unity with God, can we again become integrated and made healthy and happy. Culture and its social mores render the whole concept of sex tragic when sex is over-simplified to refer almost exclusively to the act of sexual intercourse. God wants sex to be something more.

Another useful metaphor for explaining human sexuality is that of a piano. A standard keyboard has an assortment of eighty-eight keys. All of the keys are important to have a fully functional musical instrument capable of producing beautiful songs. But what would happen if you limited the functionality of the piano, by eliminating all but two musical keys, leaving only two playable notes? The resultant two-note "song" would become immediately repetitious and quickly unsatisfying. By the same token, if we limit our concept of human sexuality to only "two notes" consisting of a "penis" and a "vagina," we severely restrict our ability to experience true intimacy and joy.

The Counselor then leaned forward slightly in his chair, as if to indicate earnestness. Then, in a serious tone, he said that part of the answer is to stop thinking in terms of *sexuality*, and to start thinking in terms of *sensuality*. He told me that by adopting a much broader and richer understanding of sex, we can more closely approach the joy that God wants human beings to experience. The Counselor said that when our sensory life is working optimally, then everything we see, feel, taste, smell, and hear is explosive with sensual stimulation; stimulation that feeds directly into the mind and generates tremendous pleasure within us. Moreover, we can experience this wonderful pleasure free of any fear, guilt, shame, or regret.

This kind of optimal sensual experience can result from everyday activities such as eating a meal with a group of friends or walking barefoot on the grass in a park on a summer day or playing a simple game of fetch with a neighbor's dog. When we live a highly-sensualized, godly lifestyle, we become totally aware of the universe and the explosive beauty that surrounds us. We can grow freer in our ability to mindfully experience and appreciate the beauty and sensory pleasure we feel throughout every moment of life. Godly sensuality is so radically different and more expansive than society's fascination with lustful sexual encounters between people. Our culture's fixation on eroticism is ultimately narrow, repetitive, disappointing, and even pathetic. Instead, God wants to grant us a *total* life experience that is full, fresh, challenging, constantly evolving, and filled with healthy excitement. The Bible challenges us to "taste and see that the Lord is good" and to seek Him as our ultimate source of life fulfillment. [68]

The Counselor told me that obsessions with sexual acts and deviant behaviors lead to numbness and the loss of feeling in the human body. He made an interesting comment about how some seventeen-year-old porn addicts suffer from erectile dysfunction, with their bodies rendered unable to respond to normal sexual stimulation. The Counselor continued by citing the work of a Canadian psychiatrist and author, Norman Doidge, M.D, who wrote a bestselling book entitled *The Brain That Changes Itself*. In his book, Dr. Doidge explains how sexual "tolerance" is not unlike that of a drug addict whose body becomes accustomed to a narcotic drug, and ultimately requires increased dosages of the drug to sustain a high level of euphoric pleasure. Similarly, Dr. Doidge describes how porn addicts develop a tolerance to increasingly graphic, and even violent, sexual imagery. Dr. Doidge goes on to explain:

> When pornographers boast that they are pushing the envelope by introducing new, harder themes, what they don't say is that they must, because their customers are building up a tolerance to the content.[69]

By sharp contrast, godly forms of sensuality result in an enhanced, self-actualized joy and much greater life satisfaction. In a way that is hard to understand or explain, God becomes our lover, and the ultimate source of our contentment. The challenge Christians face is to transcend the purely physical and the synthetic forms of pleasure that are now so widely available in our culture. Instead, Christians must look to God as the source for securing inner harmony and life fulfillment.

Beyond Sex and Sensuality—A Spiritual Model

I want to further explore this idea of a godly experience that trumps anything offered by our carnal, pill popping, recreational-sex culture. More importantly, how do we achieve non-fragmented wholeness and enjoy an intact, "unbroken mirror" existence? The Counselor sat back comfortably in his chair, as if pondering this topic. He then said the apostle Paul taught God's will was both "good" and "perfect."[70] If we accept the idea that a good and perfect creator of the universe designed a specific plan for human existence, can we not reasonably assume such a strategy for humanity would, itself, be highly satisfying for God's beloved children?

Today, even in a fallen world, the Counselor makes the bold statement that it is still possible for people to approach the kind and quality of life that God had originally planned for His human children. Moreover, the avenue for achieving such true happiness can be found through the power of the human mind. The mind, or when put into Christian terms, the human *spirit*, is our connection to God's Holy Spirit. The Counselor told me that Adam and Eve must have enjoyed a kind of sensuality that extended beyond their physical bodies. All their senses (not just their sexual instincts) must have been supernaturally heightened during their early time in the Garden of Eden, prior to the introduction of sin and the subsequent fall of humanity. In the early days of Adam and Eve, the sky, the trees, the grasses, the fragrances of the air, the taste of the water—everything Adam and Eve experienced must have seemed vibrant, orchestral, harmonic, and perfect.

The Counselor concluded that, early in their existence, Adam and Eve must have been able to transcend the limits of their physical bodies. He assumed they were able to reach into God's spiritual realm and experience amazing pleasure without guilt, fear, shame, or regret. The result must have been a lifestyle unmatched by anything today's broken society can offer using synthetic drugs, alcohol, or kinky sexual fetishes. However you choose to describe it, as either human self-actualization, optimal life fulfillment, or utopian living—these things could only have been possible for Adam and Eve through their close and ongoing personal relationship with God.

In truth, the idyllic model of joy and wholeness that the Counselor shared with me, is really something beyond sex. In fact, it is something that even transcends the broader definition of sensuality. In several places in the Bible, the Scriptures make obscure references to "the bride of Christ."[71] One interpretation is that the Christian Church is to assume the role of Christ's "bride," and that Jesus assumes the role of husband and is "married" to the individuals who compose the Christian Church. If humanity is somehow "wedded" to God through Jesus, then this creates the awkward notion of God as our husband—or worse—God as our *lover*. I understand this concept is highly uncomfortable for many people, largely because of the world's sick ideas involving sex and what it commonly means to take a "lover." But if we can put aside any unhealthy thinking, then this idea of "God as our lover" raises some interesting questions.

MODEL 2
A PATHWAY TO PLEASURE

SPIRITUALITY
⬆
SENSUALITY
⬆
SEXUALITY

Society's obsession with eroticism has caused many people to confuse sex with nurture. "Support, care, affirmation, and love are all sexualized." (Carnes, 2001, p. 110) Many people have subsequently forfeited a much broader, more satisfying sensuality in order to satisfy their raw sexual appetites. But far worse is that, with this stunted societal view of sex, most people are completely unable to make themselves available to a still higher form of enjoyment, whereby they experience God as their lover.

The Counselor said the key here is to use the higher thought processes of our human mind and spirit. If humanity could learn to truly connect with God on His terms, on a spiritual level, it would be possible for people to enjoy a kind of thinking and feeling that would extend our lives to a vast, integrated, and transcendent spiritual plane. This type of supernatural relationship with God would transform our existence into something wonderful and exciting, and so much of life would become a *wow!* experience for us. Why? Because if we could successfully live this kind of optimal lifestyle, a person could better experience union and harmony with a limitless God.

What exactly stops us from experiencing God as our lover? The answer is that we are unable to achieve a true, intimate relationship with God because we value other things more highly. We are entrenched in perverse relationships with other, more worldly lovers. We are too often distracted by the values of society, leaving little room for God in our lives. The Bible clearly warns us not to commit idolatry.[72] Yet the ultimate idolatry came long ago, when humanity first decided to abandon God. Humanity instead chose to engage in sin and to enjoy unhealthy practices. People traded perfect spiritual harmony with the Lord for what the Bible calls "thorns and thistles" and fragmentation and heartache in a broken world.[73]

Contemporary society is severely damaged and desensitized. Nowadays, some people think the fullest definition of *happiness* is achieved when male and female genitalia join together during acts of fornication. The Counselor went on to say he has more excitement and fun by watching tree leaves swaying in the wind than his sex-addicted patients have from their frequent orgies and other extreme debaucheries. The sex addicts have totally desensitized themselves, and they must now use their intelligence (housed within the mind and spirit) to return to health and wholeness. There exists, through spirituality and maintaining a personal relationship with God, an optimal life experience that can be obtained through no other means than by a close connection with the Lord of the universe.

The Counselor expresses hope when he says that he has clients who are "thirty and forty-year sex addicts and were the leaders of the eroticism movement," but have now regained peace and wholeness through spiritual means. He says these extreme sex addicts needed to give up their false ideas about satisfaction and pleasure. They needed to change their way of thinking about life. In the end, he says they report having tasted of God and have chosen not to go back to their former idols and toxic lifestyles. Lastly, the Counselor emphasized that their decision to change was *not* due to some "religious morality conversion." In other words, these career sex addicts did not suddenly find the Bible and choose the nobler path. Not at all. Instead, these former secularists decided that spiritual wholeness was more "fun" and satisfying than the sensual death that comes by engaging in many of the socially-acceptable practices of today's broken culture. Ultimately, their decision to change was born out of selfishness and self-interest. Nonetheless, they are now living happier, healthier lives by knowing God.

In spirituality, there is a pleasure that is unmatched by eroticism. Eroticism alone has its limits and "hits a ceiling" whereby it proves to be numbing and unsatisfying. We must not overdo one avenue of expression, lest we fragment and lose the holistic experience of God. The Counselor cautioned me, "Sex will die, if it is not kept subordinate to the bigger picture of sensuality—and ultimately, spirituality." Things like pornography kill the ability to feel, and ultimately cause erectile dysfunction and the loss of orgasm. We have unknowingly and unconsciously sold-off the broader sensual and spiritual experiences of life. We must now seek an expansive horizon-to-horizon knowledge of life as our preferred pathway to pleasure.

Seeking Restoration

We need to learn how to feel again. It can start with specific exercises, such as paying attention to the taste, color, smell, and texture of the foods we eat. We should also fully experience and enjoy the richness, beauty, and power of nature. Consider taking a brisk, early morning stroll amidst the lifting fog on a spring day. Exhale, and reflect upon your own frosty breath as you walk under God's majestic sky, or beneath a grove of His towering trees. Appreciate the joyous cacophony of wild songbirds, and celebrate a season of new hope as delicate cherry blossoms transform into the lush, vibrant, mature foliage of summer. Count and appreciate all the different shades of green in the leaves and the grasses.

During fall and winter, walk through a country field, or a city park, and take pleasure in the stark beauty found in the harsh, threatening gray skies of an approaching storm. Listen for the rumble of brooding, distant thunder, and feast your ears upon the sounds of the wind and the rustling breezes as they disturb the slumbering branches of the dormant trees. Breathe in the fresh scent of the air after a cleansing winter rain. Pay attention to the unique shapes of the clouds in the sky and notice the subtle nuances and beauties of nature in all its seasons. Make a conscious effort to really experience the vibrant colors, delightful smells, the physical sensations, and the sights associated with mountain or ocean vistas. Be sure to appreciate all that God's creation offers you as you seek personal restoration and wholeness. Whether you dwell in a rural countryside or within an urban forest, learn to be amazed by God's infinite creativity as it is demonstrated throughout nature; a nature that offers you peace and can serve as a tremendous source of mental and emotional renewal.

Savor the positive experiences of life, no matter how small or insignificant they may at first appear. Whether it is listening to soothing music that puts you into a calm mood or participating in a child's "pretend tea party" which brings out your own fun-loving inner child—seize upon the full range of healthy pleasures life has to offer. Do not scoff at these simple suggestions, but understand that opportunities to experience godly sensuality may take unexpected forms. Amazing sensual experiences can be had by gazing out of an airplane window at thirty thousand feet during business travel, or by enjoying the aroma of fresh bread baking in your kitchen, or through the flash of insight you might gain while reading a Dostoevsky novel. The point here is to shake off the numbness and the deadness of your former existence. Philippians 4:8 (TLB) encourages us to fix our thoughts "on what is true and good and right" and to "think about things that are pure and lovely, and to dwell on the fine," good things in life.

Later, you can begin to expand and properly develop your experience of sexuality. For married people, try physical, but not overtly sexual touching of your spouse. Do this frequently, maybe even a hundred times per day! Furthermore, by focusing on sensuality and sensual contact during your sexual activity, you can stimulate oxytocin and vasopressin (natural mate bonding hormones) as well as pheromone production within the body. Beta-endorphins, which are stronger painkillers than morphine and that positively affect mood and attitude, will eventually begin to naturally be produced by the body as your mind becomes healthier. Moreover, in time, your old negative images and remembrances of unhealthy sexual experiences will fade and disappear from memory. Use the principle of neuroplasticity to establish new and beneficial pathways in both your lower and upper brain. The process of healing is incremental and can take one or two years or longer.

A Very Personal Example

Lastly, allow me to conclude this section by sharing some personal thoughts and experiences from my own marriage. For over a decade, from the beginning of my relationship with my wife, we had always carried some vague concerns about the "normalcy and adequacy" of our sex life. I think both of us had expressed disappointments, of one sort or another, at various times over the years. But my therapy sessions with the Counselor changed everything. Therapy afforded me a totally fresh perspective for gauging the quality of my physical relationship with my spouse. Today, I believe that my wife and I have achieved something very similar to what Adam and Eve likely enjoyed in their marriage relationship, before the fall of humanity. In general, when we interact outside of the bedroom, my spouse and I become like the "little kids" whom Jesus talked about in Matthew 18:3 (NIV). Jesus had told his disciples, "Truly I tell you, unless you change and become like little children, you will never enter the kingdom of heaven."

In retrospect, I think my wife and I had been living correctly all along, but we made the mistake of listening to the lies and false claims of society. We allowed the world to deceive us, and ultimately to rob us of some of our joy, earlier in our marriage. For years, we measured our relationship's success, both in and out of the bedroom, in the wrong ways. In truth, my spouse and I have always cherished our time spent together. As I mentioned above, when we interact as a married couple, we bring out the inner child in one another and become the fun-loving kids whom Jesus called the "greatest in the kingdom of heaven."[74] Whether my wife and I spend time feeding stale bread to a team of ducks at the local lake, or whether we drive out into the countryside and enjoy an old-fashioned farmer's hayride at the Harvest Festival— we always manage to have our own unique and silly brand of fun. We thoroughly enjoy our time together and make many beautiful memories. We are crafting a rich and happy married life.

Moreover, when we finally retreat into the bedroom, our lovemaking is tender, emotionally-charged, and utterly heartfelt and genuine. We abstain from prescription drugs, sex toys, or any artificial or perverse indulgences. Yes, I suppose the physical nature of our union would, in fact, be somewhat different if we were both twenty-five years younger. But for where we are in our current stage of life, I think we are approaching God's intent in our sexual relationship. In bed with my spouse, I find myself quickly awash in powerful emotions of love and admiration for her. In such close physical proximity, I stare into her beautiful face and reflect upon the years we have spent together. In my mind, I blissfully recall and savor our full and complete history as a couple.

During such private moments, we celebrate what C.S. Lewis called a "transcendental relation." Such a relationship is built upon what Lewis described as a foundation of affection, fidelity, goodwill, and loyalty to a partnership.[75] Our marriage is part of a broader fabric of experience that my wife and I have jointly woven and shared; our marriage has been a key to making a great life. We have crafted an amazing friendship; it is a sacred trust inspired and approved by God Himself. I can barely comprehend the miracle of it all. At times, the thoughts and past remembrances are too poignant and too joyously painful for me to endure without an onslaught of tears. While in bed, I begin to rapidly and repeatedly kiss my wife all over her precious face. I cannot stop myself. Again and again I offer her sharp, staccato, kisses. And soon she begins to blush and smile and swoon like a young girl, in response to my effusive and persistent affections. "My Kissing Machine," she finally whispers softly to me—a pet name she still uses today, just as she did years ago when we were a dating couple and everything was so new, exciting, and untested in our budding relationship.

Recently, I have begun to glimpse the appearance of a few silver hairs on my wife's head, and these serve only to punctuate and emphasize the span of time and life that we have shared. I love my spouse's silver hairs. They are each as trophies to me; trophies she earned during hard and good times, through tears and laughter, and during victory and loss. I am reminded of our marriage vows: "for better and for worse, for richer and for poorer, in sickness and in health, to love and to cherish… 'til death do us part." I cannot believe how blessed I am. My cup runneth over. What I describe here is how I now view the godly ideal of love, sex, and of a relationship for a married couple. It is wondrous. It is real. It is an unspeakable joy. It is a manifestation of God's glory and power, and it will last a lifetime.

Eric Roderiques

More on God as Our Lover: A Supernatural Vision

Upon completing the first manuscript of this book, I remained somewhat dissatisfied with our earlier discussions of "God as our lover." To me, the concept remained somewhat intangible, or at the very least, incomplete. But then God gave me a simple, yet powerful vision that helped make things clearer for me. I understand that many people will immediately become skeptical if I talk of having received a "vision from God." I wish I could say that I experienced something ground shaking involving the Almighty. But what I saw in my mind was quite simple and seemed to lack fanfare. Yet, I think the symbolism expressed in the following imagery is how our Lord wants His relationship with humanity to be understood. I was not alone in this vision, but I also saw my wife depicted. I saw both my wife and I portrayed as little children, probably around the age of five or six years old. The child metaphor is essential.

Here, briefly, is the vision God presented to me: Represented as a pair of youngsters, I saw my wife and I playing together innocently in an open space; a large field of grass infused with bright daylight and surrounded by trees with a canopy of blue sky overhead. We both suddenly glimpsed a man standing nearby. We knew this man to be Jesus, and so we immediately ran towards him and jumped into his outstretched arms. He promptly and happily welcomed and held us firmly, as would any loving father. My wife squealed and rejoiced with the happy abandon of an excited young girl, while I boyishly attempted to engage the Lord of the universe in a playful wrestling match. All the while, Jesus seemed to thoroughly enjoy the loving interaction with two of his little children.

I think this simple rendering symbolizes the kind and quality of optimal living that every person should seek. Happiness in life is all about forming a childlike and close relationship with God. It is for such an intimate relationship we were created, and it is through such a relationship that we will discover our ultimate worth, joy, and fulfillment. Nothing else can complete us, and nothing else will better allow us to reach our maximum potential than to know our heavenly father and to know Him well.

Eroticism is for Now

Perhaps we need to keep a proper perspective when we consider the topic of human sexuality and eroticism. In the end, these things are fundamental, but I think they are also very temporary accommodations. Certainly, God had a plan and a purpose when He invented human sexuality; His intent is for more than animalistic copulation between people. Clearly, God's purpose is for married individuals to experience healthy pleasure, and to procreate and thereby perpetuate the human species here on earth. But I think there is more to it. The foundation of godly human sexuality seems to be something *spiritual*. Sex is supposed to be good and wonderful as it is described in the Bible's Song of Solomon. Yes, sex is clearly an important part of this life. But often it has also become confused and made sick by our fallen culture. The Bible warns against abusing our sexuality. Beginning in 1 Corinthians 6:16, the Bible says:

> There's more to sex than mere skin on skin. Sex is as much spiritual mystery as physical fact. As written in Scripture, "The two become one." Since we want to become spiritually one with the Master, we must not pursue the kind of sex that avoids commitment and intimacy, leaving us more lonely than ever. (*The Message*)

It would appear the more we grow spiritually, the less we should concern ourselves with the things of *this* world. Now, I am not saying we can ignore our responsibilities here on earth, but we must also look forward to our ultimate place in heaven. We should begin work now to grow in character so that we may better understand the spiritual mysteries of God. There is a fundamental difference between "living in the spirit" and "living in the flesh." Sexuality and eroticism are significant realities during our mortal existence on this planet, but we will presumably encounter greater truths once we achieve heaven and become immortal beings who possess spiritual bodies.

"Be perfect" was a command given to us by Jesus Christ.[76] It is God's vision to eventually render His people into spiritual creatures capable of perfection. C.S. Lewis pondered and speculated about how, one day in the future, God will make the feeblest and filthiest of His followers into "dazzling, radiant, immortal creatures, pulsating all through with such energy and joy and wisdom and love" as we cannot presently imagine. Lewis went on to say how the Lord will someday transform each of His people into a bright, "stainless mirror which reflects back to God perfectly" God's own limitless power and delightful kindness, albeit on a much smaller scale.[77] Irrespective of whether this amazing change takes place in some distant heavenly future, or begins sooner within the confines of this present life, God promises incredible transformation and growth for those who believe in Him and seek to know Him. The apostle Paul quoted the Old Testament scripture from Isaiah and talked about how no secular eye has seen, no worldly ear has heard, and no fleshly heart has imaged the good things God has prepared for those who love Him. There are mysteries of God's mercy and grace that can only be revealed to those who fully live the Christian lifestyle.[78]

To us now it may seem crazy and extreme, but in the Bible, God made special provision for those wanting to be closest to Him during their time here on earth. At the end of Matthew 19, Jesus talked about a group of people who could abstain from sex "for the sake of God's Kingdom."[79] Similarly, the apostle Paul later talked about marriage and advocated it for those who otherwise would, "Burn with passion."[80] But, as for himself, Paul devoted all his energies and attention to building his personal relationship with

God. For this reason, during his Christian ministry, Paul chose to remain unmarried and to abstain from sexual activity.

In Matthew 22:30 (NIV), Jesus explained what life in heaven will one day be like. He said that, in heaven, people will "neither marry nor be given in marriage; they will be like the angels in heaven." Obviously, in our contemporary earthly society, celibacy is not a very popular lifestyle option for many to consider. But once we move beyond this life and are given new, spiritual bodies, we will no longer worry about matters of species procreation or sexual satisfaction or eroticism. We will have no need, and probably feel little desire for carnal, physical relationships once we become immortal, spirit-beings. Again, it appears there is a far greater pleasure awaiting us as we progress and become "fully spirit," and connect with God in the way He wants us to know and love Him. Once we reach heaven, the only remaining marriage relationship will be our marriage to God.

Perfect Peace

But what about during this life on earth? As living human beings, can we somehow begin to experience an ultimate pleasure that is better than anything sexual eroticism offers? The Bible gives us an answer in the Old Testament's book of Isaiah. Isaiah 26:3 begins:

> You [God] will keep in perfect peace those whose minds are steadfast, because they trust in you.[81]

The above phrase, "perfect peace," is translated from the Hebrew to include the word *shalom*. We will talk more about the Jewish understanding of *shalom* in a later chapter. But for now, understand that the idea of achieving inner peace runs throughout the entire Bible, and is also translated into the Greek language.[82] For example, in the New Testament's Greek translation, the apostle Paul said:

> Let the peace of Christ rule in your hearts, since as members of one body you were called to peace. And be thankful.[83]

Paul further taught:

> And the peace of God, which transcends all understanding, will guard your hearts and your minds in Christ Jesus.[84]

Jesus, himself, spoke of the importance of achieving ultimate, spiritual peace, when he said:

> I have told you these things, so that in me you may have peace. In this world you will have trouble. But take heart! I have overcome the world.[85]

Think about why some people use sexual activity as a temporary escape from the stresses, tensions, and problems of life. Eroticism experienced through inappropriate thoughts, practices, or relationships offers a false kind of "quick fix" distraction and relief from the troubles and hurts of this broken world. But eroticism outside the context of marriage provides only a temporary sort of pleasure. When people abuse their sexuality to self-medicate pain, the result can often be feelings of guilt, shame, and regret—which only serve to increase suffering.

In sharp contrast to what is available through worldly practices such as fornication and adultery, the Bible promises a far superior path to pleasure. The preferred approach to a happy life requires that we build a strong personal relationship with God. Moreover, in the above scriptural passage, Isaiah 26:3 tells us that a right relationship with the Lord depends upon our "steadfast mind" that is fixed upon the truth of our Creator. The Counselor said that it is only through a relentless trust and reliance in Jesus Christ that people can control their primal thinking. Remember, it is the primal brain that often causes us to make destructive decisions and to engage in inappropriate behaviors that place a distance between God and us. If we are ruled by our primal brains, we will most likely be robbed of our supreme happiness, peace, and wholeness.

Review of Counseling Session 4

1. Excellence of character does not mean we need to be perfect in this lifetime. The Christian system of belief holds that the only perfect, sinless person to ever live was Jesus Christ. While we strive to change our bad habits into healthier ways of living, we need to show ourselves mercy when we occasionally stumble. God is pleased with our honest efforts to improve. He knows that we are human. He sympathizes with our struggles and our imperfections, and He stands ready to forgive us if we sometimes make poor choices.
2. Unleash the power of prayer in your life. Reach out to God and make Him the source of your hope for a better future.
3. Satan wants to strike a blow against God by corrupting the lives of God's much-beloved children. The devil is jealous of God's good plan for humanity. Satan is jealous of God's good plan for *you*.
4. Often there is pain that comes as part of a healing process. We can experience "withdrawal symptoms" when we try to change our bad habits. But the discomfort of withdrawal from bad habits fades over time as we become healthier in both mind and body.
5. Our ability to enjoy normal, healthy pleasures can be compromised if we engage in unnatural habits that distort our expectations and our ability to feel.
6. Our goal should be to move beyond the false expectations of our shattered culture and to adopt a spiritual model for living that has God at its center. Our motivation should be to seek after what the Bible calls *perfect peace*.

Counseling Session 5
Anger Management

At harvest time Cain brought the Lord a gift of his farm produce, and Abel brought the fatty cuts of meat from his best lambs, and presented them to the Lord. And the Lord accepted Abel's offering, but not Cain's. This made Cain both dejected and very angry, and his face grew dark with fury. "Why are you angry?" the Lord asked him. "Why is your face so dark with rage? It can be bright with joy if you will do what you should! But if you refuse to obey, watch out. Sin is waiting to attack you, longing to destroy you. But you can conquer it!"

Genesis 4:3-7 (TLB)

It was during my fifth therapy session that the Counselor explained how the practices described in this book may be adapted to address a host of other behavioral and emotional problems, beyond issues of sexual purity. The Joshua Protocol, in particular, is a highly adaptable approach to prayer and can be used to confront different areas of human hurt, pain, or dysfunction. (Appendix 1 of this text lists numerous examples of how to utilize the Joshua Protocol for different situations.) The concept of neuroplasticity is central to understanding how the human mind, with its higher consciousness, can successfully reshape the apparatus that is the physical brain.

Let us now expand our discussion and consider how the Joshua Protocol helps us tackle the problem of anger management.

Therapist and trauma specialist, H. Norman Wright, explains in his book, *A Better Way to Think: How Positive Thoughts Can Change Your Life*, that unchecked, explosive, and destructive anger typically comes from three sources. These three sources are the feelings of hurt, fear, or frustration we encounter through life events or through our personal circumstances.[86] But we can be mindful of such feelings so to better understand why we are angry at a given moment. Moreover, we can use the Joshua Protocol to invoke the power of godly prayer to curb and regulate our uncontrolled or dysfunctional feelings of anger.

I think the story of Cain and Abel, as described in the Bible's book of Genesis, offers three quick truths about anger. First, problems associated with anger have faced humanity since the beginning of time. Second, uncontrolled anger can result in disastrous consequences for us and those around us, as the Genesis story illustrates: Cain's rage triggered him to ruthlessly murder his younger brother, Abel. This sudden, brutal act forever changed the course of history for Cain and his descendants. Third, chapter 4 in the book of Genesis tells us that through God's grace and supernatural power, a way exists for people to properly regulate their feelings of anger.

Let me be clear when I say anger is a normal human emotion; it is only when people's rage goes out-of-control and becomes too frequent, too explosive, or otherwise harmful that difficulties arise. The Bible also tells us that God, Himself, feels anger. But our Lord sets the proper example for us, by being "slow to anger."[87] We, too, should seek to moderate how we express angry feelings. We would be wise to try and neutralize any old life narrative that triggers new instances of explosive or counterproductive anger within us. But one problem with accomplishing this goal is that we live in an increasingly angry world, where violence and hatred appear to be on the rise. In such an atmosphere, people are continuously absorbing the rage and hurt that surrounds them in society. This ongoing negativity threatens to infect each of us and to render us angry.

The Bible warns that holding onto anger is dangerous in the way it hinders our ability to love others.[88] Put simply, if we are filled with anger and rage, then we are less likely to show love and respect to those around us. Moreover, by making us less loving, anger threatens to nullify the positive power of our spiritual faith. This is to say, anger can hinder our personal relationship with God. The biblical proof is found when the apostle Paul instructed the Galatian people that it is only faith "working through love" that makes a person right with God.[89] In 1 Corinthians 13:2 (NIV), Paul continues by saying:

> If I have the gift of prophecy and can fathom all mysteries and all knowledge, and if I have a faith that can move mountains, but do not have love, I am nothing.

Before we can achieve a clear victory over our bad habits, negative thoughts, or our compulsions, we must first control any unresolved anger and resentment that may be deeply rooted within us. I will begin this short discussion on anger management by defining a couple of key terms that the Counselor used during my therapy sessions.

Medical anger—This is something closely tied to our human physiology and primal brains. This type of anger is a normal and natural response to physical stress and pain. If somebody physically or emotionally hurts you (e.g., hits, slaps, bites, chokes, insults, demeans, etc.) and causes you pain or harm, then the natural instinctive response is one of anger and perhaps even a sudden, reflexive backlash against the attacker. The Counselor says that medical anger is not premeditated and it happens against our will.

Furthermore, it is an entirely reasonable, understandable, and acceptable manifestation of our emotions at a given instant.

The Counselor asked me to consider the real-life example of a mother who sells her daughter into child prostitution. Later in her life, as an adult, an anger response on the part of the surviving daughter is perfectly rational. But the victimized adult daughter would be wise to separate the harmful act from the person responsible for it. This is to say, if the daughter continues to hate her mother for past abuses, then the daughter loses her relationship with her mother for both now and the future. However, if the daughter hates only what her mother did to her in the past (i.e., the pimping and resultant sexual assault, pain, violence, exploitation, etc.) then the daughter can preserve a valuable relationship with her parent. In the next section of this book, we will discuss how parent-child relationships are essential in maintaining a person's emotional health and well-being.

The key is for the surviving daughter to understand that her mother, most likely, did not want to exploit her own child. Most probably, the mother was somehow compelled by society or the mother's environment or her own personal history, life narrative, or emotional hurts. Perhaps the mother had, herself, been sexually abused as a child and was merely passing on some damaged emotional baggage to her daughter. It is reasonable for the daughter to subsequently hate the "disease" of her mother's poisoned emotional conditioning. But, it is not advisable that the daughter hate her mother. We must learn to distinguish between an individual's "who" (a person's fundamental identity) and their "do" (their actions). The real individual, the "who," is a much-loved child of God. Their spirit is built to resemble that of Jesus Christ. It is only their actions, or their "do," that may be sick, hurtful to others, or otherwise wrong.

Spiritual anger—As human beings, we are not qualified, the Counselor said "not good enough," to play God and to pass judgments upon other people. We cannot, for all time and eternity, damn or otherwise *judge* our brothers and sisters because they have hurt us. Judgment is the purview of God, not of men. God reserves the right of retribution for Himself when He said, "It is mine to avenge; I will repay."[90] If we try to pick-up the sword of vengeance that belongs only to God, we lose favor with the Lord.

Case Study in Betrayal & Anger Management: The Story of *A*

I wanted to share a personal experience with the Counselor. It was an event that had taken place much earlier in my life, shortly after college. Although this incident took place decades ago, it continued to weigh heavily upon my mind. I had suffered a horrible betrayal in business by a close female confidante, whom I will simply call A. A's background and upbringing make an interesting story. A had been born outside of the United States, in a developing country overseas. Her biological parents were financially destitute, and A's earliest memories were ones of severe hardship and deprivation, which resulted from her family's poverty. At just eight years of age, A was given away by her biological parents to a married couple of American religious missionaries. The Americans already had a large family of their own, consisting of six children. With her young eyes, A watched how the American missionaries initially bristled at the thought of an international adoption. But A's biological parents begged the Americans and threatened to sell A into child prostitution if the American missionaries refused to take custody of her. Ultimately, the Americans relented and adopted A into their family, and returned with the child to the United States. But early on, A was keenly aware that she had been an unwanted burden to both her biological birth parents and to her new American family. This knowledge profoundly impacted A's emotional development as she grew, and it ultimately shaped her conduct as an adult.

Many years later, I met A when we shared the same employer and worked together professionally. We both started with an established and highly-respected company and were tasked to jointly manage a complex business unit. Unfortunately, after just a few months of working together, the whole business environment changed. Soon, the task of operations management became stressful and uncertain for us. During this time, A began to feel pressure and fear as our business unit faltered and our career tenure with the company was called into question. During this tumultuous season, A sought to insulate and protect her livelihood from the threats. She did so by sacrificing me to them. Her betrayal soon left me emotionally devastated and unemployed.

After hearing further details of my story, the Counselor offered a rough clinical impression of what might have prompted A to act against me. He told me that everyone is subject to their environment, especially as it relates to the bond between a child and his or her mother. The topic of "attachment theory" comes into play here. Normal mother-child nurturing was taken away from A, at a young age. This type of situation can create an imbalance in a person's emotional makeup. The Counselor urged me to think of human emotions as being represented by the letter "Y" with its two upper branches. One of these upper branches represents the *parasympathetic nervous system*, which is our "safe and secure" (i.e., our optimistic or happy) branch that anchors and stabilizes our emotions. This part of A's emotional makeup was arrested in its growth when her impoverished birth parents were unable to properly value her as a person. A was sacrificed for the sake of her birth family and sent to live with strangers in America. Ultimately, this break most likely created an arrested development of her parasympathetic nervous system, which is responsible for regulating a person's feeling of joy, as well as their sense of safety, stability, and peace.

What most likely grew, and ultimately dominated A's personality, was her *sympathetic nervous system*. This sympathetic nervous system is the "fight or flight" (i.e., the cautious, fearful, or sad) instincts of a person. The Counselor told me that A probably became "threat dominant" and "opportunity passive" in her personality makeup. Again, using the letter "Y" metaphor, we can say that A's upper branch that represented her happiness and positive outlook on life had failed to grow because of her childhood trauma. And later, as an adult, A's emotional makeup remained uneven and stunted with only one fully formed branch of her "Y"—the sad branch—being fully developed. All this is to say that A's primal instincts for survival grew and ultimately came to dominate her personality. A lacked a fundamental balance in her happy and sad emotions.

The Counselor indicated that "sympathetic nervous system dominant" (sad) people tend to be Type-A perfectionists. As a coping mechanism to cover their feelings of inadequacy, these people often become hyper-moralistic and sick, as they unconsciously strive to look good and be good in the eyes of others and society. All their energy is devoted to maintaining a heightened level of alertness as they defend against anything that could possibly go wrong around them. Ultimately, such a lifestyle is unsustainable, and these kinds of people tend to bleed-out emotionally, and finally crash. These workaholics have problems in middle age, due to their imbalanced perspective. They exhaust themselves trying to maintain their obsessive masks of perfection. In the instance involving the external threats that imperiled both A and me, she went into a full combat, defensive mode. A's primal lower-brain bastardized her higher-level intelligence to build a perfectly structured and perfectly invented defense. But her brain was unable to consider the disastrous impact that her actions had upon me.

Transforming Anger & Hurt

The Counselor provided me some additional background information. He went on to say his job is to be positive and to help his clients understand the challenges they face so they may better conquer and rise above their pain. He indicated how he regularly invokes the name, power, grace, and the mercy of God as both an encouragement and as a spiritual means of healing his clients' hurts. The Counselor offered me the illustration of child abuse victims. He said that in cases of child abuse, the mental and emotional damage suffered is as real and significant as the physical trauma that a victim would experience in, for example, a severe automobile accident. But in the case of a child abuse victim, the psychological damage can result in a legacy of anger, fear, or low self-esteem that can last a lifetime. Treatment must be sought to try and repair the situation.

The goal of treatment is to empower the mind, which is housed within the upper brain, to assign a fresh and positive meaning to past abuse. But can a person assign a "positive" meaning to horrific acts that took place in their lives? Through the process of neuroplasticity, we now know that the physical processes of the brain can be changed. It is possible to assign new meanings to old experiences. Much like Jesus, we can transform stagnant water into a sweet wine.[91] The Counselor uses the analogy of an oyster that is able to fashion a beautiful pearl from an irritating grain of embedded sand. In the Counselor's analogy, the oyster initially suffers pain and irritation when its soft tissues are invaded by an outside nuisance. But the oyster quickly responds by encapsulating the source of its pain with a lustrous nacre, until a beautiful pearl is formed from the grain of sand.

The cries of our own pain and hurt, coming out of the lower primal thinking, are legitimate and real. But we can empower the upper brain's intelligence (i.e., our mind and spirit) as the preferred ruler over our bodies. A spiritual mind can gain dominance over a physical brain and all its base instincts. Moreover, a spiritual mind can structure a better understanding of the causes of the medical anger and the hurts it suffers. This becomes possible if we can make better sense of why our abuse happened in the first place.

We need to understand the real background root of our present circumstances. Such knowledge helps us to better manage and regulate our anger and feelings. It can be like putting our anger into a box, or a cage, so we can take control of it. The process of gaining mastery over anger and pain takes a considerable amount of time, at least one or two years, and may require professional counseling.

> <u>Author's Note</u>: *This book is a primer on concepts and healing approaches found in the Bible. It is not a substitute for professional mental health intervention. In the event of a mental health emergency, I encourage readers to seek professional counseling immediately.*

But the final outcome of this process is the dismissal of our past hurts. Through God's grace, mercy, and restorative power, we mentally separate the terrible facts of past events from our increasing spiritual wholeness of today. We firmly come to understand that we are much loved by God. Such a greater reality transcends the upheavals we suffered. Moreover, we can see our tormentors for whom they really are. Those who have hurt us are, themselves, tragically broken. There is an old saying that applies here: "Hurting people hurt people." While we might not choose to excuse our enemies and tormentors, we can, nonetheless, better understand them and perhaps even learn to pity them as troubled creatures. Armed with this truth, we can change our whole interpretation of our pasts. We can suddenly view our experiences through a more positive lens. Knowledge is power. We can become capable of interpreting personal tragedy more favorably, even triumphantly. We survived our circumstances, we overcame them, and now we are stronger and wiser because of them. We won.

In terms of our spiritual development, we can use past negativity as a means of building a closer and more personal relationship with the creator of the universe. Christian psychiatrist, Dwight L. Carlson, M.D., encourages us to dissipate our anger constructively; he suggests that we cleanse ourselves of anger by maintaining a robust prayer life.[92] By leaning on God as we work to understand and address our areas of pain, we can find a greater closeness with the Lord. As we conquer our challenges, we can correctly say we have transformed our bad experiences and reclaimed them as good outcomes when we use our damaged life narratives to shape better relationships with God. We can use the past to instill positive character traits within ourselves for the future. We can leverage the former poison of our life history, and use it to build a better person for tomorrow. We can exploit past hurts to manifest love, joy, peace, patience, kindness, goodness, faithfulness, gentleness, and self-control for the time ahead. This "fruit of the spirit" is what the apostle Paul talked about in Galatians 5:22 of the Bible. By harnessing the transformative power of God, we can achieve in ourselves a closer spiritual resemblance to Jesus Christ.

Moving Beyond the Incident with A

How might I make the betrayal episode I experienced with A into something transformational and positive in my life? How might I make such an unpleasant "grain of sand" episode into a "pearl" of character development? Using the Joshua Protocol, I can begin by saying the act of betrayal was not really A's intent against me, but was a result of her life conditioning after the abandonments A suffered as a young child. The Counselor went on to talk about something he called one of the most brilliant theories of psychology. Earlier, we mentioned the concept of *attachment theory*. In the 1970s, attachment theory was developed in England by Dr. John Bowlby, and later refined by Dr. Bowlby's colleague, Dr. Mary Ainsworth of Canada.

For our purposes here, attachment theory explains the vital role of mother-child bonding in the growth and development of a child. Well-illustrated in my story of A and her birth mother, the applications of attachment theory have today been further validated through the research into neuroplasticity and the understanding that the human mind and brain are adaptable. The main point is that we can understand the root cause of A's disloyalty toward me. A's parasympathetic nervous system had become stunted, and she grew-up emotionally unstable into adulthood. I can honestly say, "*It was not really her* who hurt me." Her hostile behavior was a result of past life events that were beyond A's control.

The Secret to Super-Charged Healing: Reasoning Faith

The Counselor encouraged me to continue to grapple with my feelings as they related to the story of A. He said, "Eric, you are reasoning this out. You are using your higher-level thinking, your upper, non-primal brain and your mind. By doing so, you are getting healthier by turning your painful, emotional wound into a beautiful and valuable pearl of wisdom and life transformation." The Counselor went on to say that if I would then add the word *faith* into the equation, and bring God into this reasoning process, my results would become truly life-changing. God has the power to reshape and translate reality. He can rewrite every wrong in our lives and transform every horrific Good Friday nightmare that happens to us. He can convert our horrible Good Fridays into glorious "Easter Sunday mornings" of new life, blessings, celebration, and unspeakable joy. The Bible says all things are possible for God.[93]

If we tap into God's limitless power and combine His supernatural ability with our own upper brain's capacity for reason and good judgment, the results can be significant. When God adds His narrative and power to our healthy emotional and cognitive state, we can more easily accept any direction our lives may take. Suddenly, we benefit from an overarching grace that gives us greater hope and peace. Godly *grace* can best be described as an undeserved, unearned, or unmerited favor.[94] God's grace empowers us to overrule every unpleasant "fact" or incident that befalls us in life, so that life's hurts and indignities may be put into better perspective, and not limit our pursuit of healing and wellness. Armed with an improved perspective, we can more readily change the course of our lives so that everything works for God's greater good. We can possess overcoming faith and achieve greater life success if we start with a solid "reasoning faith."

Think of reasoning faith as a sort of cocktail. That is to say, reasoning faith mixes humanity's technical and scientific knowledge with the supernatural power of God's spirituality. Such a potent combination can super-charge our mental and emotional healing processes. But to be successful, we must move beyond religiosity or false cultural Christianity that consists of superficial role-playing on Sunday mornings at church. If we go deeper and accept Christianity as a total and comprehensive lifestyle, God's truth can help us to overcome the trials and challenges of life. Much like the Old Testament story of Shadrach, Meshach, and Abednego, we can enjoy a much greater confidence that we will safely navigate the fiery gauntlets of a challenging world and remain unhurt—not even smelling like smoke.[95] Please note that such comprehensive and satisfying life changes usually do not happen overnight, and they require a life-long commitment and an ongoing dedication to maintaining a prayerful and close personal relationship with God.

We can develop a healthy dependency upon the power of the Lord. We will undoubtedly make mistakes in life, as will the people around us. This is unavoidable. But God is all-knowing, so when He adds His infinite power to our imperfect efforts, our inadequacies suddenly become adequate. An overwhelming grace befalls us; a supernatural power takes charge of us and softens every harsh fact in life. Life, itself, is rewritten to our advantage. Life will become better, even during our ongoing challenges and disappointments that will always be a part of human existence. Romans 8:28 tells us that everything works for good when under the control of God. Maybe the events of our early years were grossly unfair and presented us with terrific challenges to overcome. The Lord of the universe can help us overcome early bad luck, misfortune, mistreatment, or any injury suffered. Looking forward, our goal should be to ensure that the remainder of our life narrative is positive and that our biography concludes with a strong ending. Frankly, God is not so much concerned about how you started your life, but He is very interested in how you will finish it.

Applying the Joshua Protocol to the Case of A

Let us take one final look at the case study involving A. By using the four steps of the Joshua Protocol, we can better understand how to respond when others hurt us. It is important to have a strategy in place for whenever we need healing in the area of our emotions. Let us review the steps of the Protocol, one-by-one:

STEP ONE: We can start by realizing that A's actions were *not really her*, but instead resulted from her prior life conditioning. We already discussed how, due to her abandonment as a child, A grew to operate out of her animalistic, primal lower brain. As an adult, she was trapped in a defensive "fight or flight" way of thinking. In response, I need to mindfully acknowledge how I was unjustly treated when I worked alongside A. But, I should also confirm in my own mind that, "I am OK, what I feel is normal medical anger. My emotions are a reasonable response to what happened in my past." The feelings of rage and anger and sadness are *not really me*, but a valid response coming from my primal, lower brain. I should then think to myself: "Yes, I was hurt by A, but I am overcoming it. God's love will take care of me. The past is finished, and the future will be better."

STEP TWO: Consider *forgiveness*. Understand that God has already forgiven A. Irrespective of whether A is a professed Christian or not, God still loves her. The Counselor explained to me the concept of *imago Dei*, which is translated as the "image of God." This Latin term in theology addresses a fundamental relationship between God and humanity. The term is found in Genesis 1:27 where, "God created man in his own image," and the phrase *imago Dei* suggests the idea that humans are somehow fashioned to resemble God in their intellectual, moral, and spiritual nature. If it is true that humans share God's own spiritual qualities, then this should extend to how humans love each other. For example, if I believe that God loves A and is predisposed to granting her unmerited favor and mercy, then I should similarly respond to A, irrespective of how she treated me. At this point you might think, "Hey, wait a minute. Are you saying God forgives everybody, and He expects us to forgive everyone too?" What about those who have not sought forgiveness or accepted Christianity? What about infamous people like Adolph Hitler or Joseph Stalin? Did God also love and forgive Hitler and Stalin through this doctrine of *imago Dei*?

To try and answer these questions, meditate on Jesus' statement from the cross: "Father, forgive them, for they do not know what they are doing."[96] And also consider Jesus' quick rebuke of the apostle Peter, when Peter tried to adopt a judgmental tone against the apostle John.[97] We are unfit to judge other people. Moreover, we cannot put God into a box. God's ways are always higher than our ways.[98] When it comes to difficult questions like whether *specific* people will face judgment before the Lord, or whether they are forgiven of their sins—we cannot absolutely answer such questions. Only God can. But in tragic cases like that of A, I should hope for the best when it comes to her relationship with the Lord. To finally resolve my old feelings of anger and hurt, I must adopt an attitude and belief that embraces the idea that God has made a way to forgive A for her past hurtful behavior towards me."[99]

More importantly, I must understand and trust that God has also forgiven *me*. Rather than focus on God's judgment of others, I need be more interested in my own good standing with the Lord. That is to say, I should be more concerned about my own righteousness. "Righteousness" is simply a fancy religious term that means being "right," or in good standing, with God. Fortunately, I believe I am forgiven. If I had *any* role to play in causing A to oppose me, I am sorry, and God has released me from any blame. God has forgiven me for any shortcomings that may have possibly triggered A's attacks against me.

Additionally, I will process my own medical anger, using my increased and broadened understanding of the situation, until my pain (the grain of sand) is transformed into a trophy (a pearl) that I can look upon victoriously. This will give me a success in life, and it will become a chance for love to overcome hate. I will let A go. I will feel love for her, and if I cannot, I will choose to exercise love and forgiveness for her in my upper brain. Once my mind decides to forgive, I will begin to exert deliberate effort to show a loving attitude towards A within my upper brain, and eventually, my genuine feelings will follow. I will choose to agree with this belief in forgiveness until the real feelings catch up with my professions. As a result of this conscious effort, I will start to heal throughout my entire being.

STEP THREE: The result of my efforts to forgive A, and to move on with my life, will be sweet *fellowship* with God that can overrule everything that is evil or bad from the past. The Counselor urged me to celebrate with God and to think of prayer time as party time. My thought process should be something like: "Dear God, we did it again; we overcame evil with good! We forgave A for what she did to me. I now have an attitude that allows me to celebrate the victories of life, both large and small, along with you, Lord. My victory in successfully responding to the episode involving A is a huge and magnificent breakthrough. Thank you, Lord."

Spending time with God and having a close personal relationship with Him covers my life with pearls, which result by transforming the painful grains of sand found throughout my life narrative. God loves the fact that I am trying to get healthier. His friendship with me offsets the bad things in my life. It is His goodness that will vanquish the evil I have experienced. By choosing a lifestyle of prayerful fellowship with God, I can ultimately overwhelm badness with goodness and change the whole course of my future. The Counselor told me that when people interact with God on a regular basis, an individual's personality becomes "good dominant" and the person begins to experience greater joy. Thankfulness should be a central focus of our prayer lives, and we must radiate thankfulness to God during all forms of prayer, whether we are reading, meditating, or even singing before the Lord. If you are not thankful for what you already have in life, why should God give you more to be dissatisfied about? Find something for which you can give God praise.

STEP FOUR: The *discipline* portion involves our thanks to God as He walks us through the painful process of our getting better. The road to joy can be a tough trek. Early in our Christian walk, perhaps we are not able to see the joy. New Christians may see and feel only the hard-edged thorns and pain of discipleship. There is a painful transition associated with the process of neuroplasticity as the mind is physically reshaped and made better. When put into a Christian context, we have already mentioned how the "crucifixion of the flesh" is something that the apostle Paul struggled with routinely.[100] In dealing with his temptations, Paul described the experience as an ongoing process of painful growth and maturation. At one point, Paul made a reference to how he "died daily" to the temptations of the world.[101]

Our bad habits will not go away easily. Godly discipline hurts, but not because God is angry with us or wants to punish us. The discipline hurts because God is targeting the evil that is intermingled within us. God plans to refashion His children, so to create new people who possess a new and better nature.[102] But, again, do not confuse this with Godly anger or punishment. Like a cancer patient who receives radiation treatments, the radiation unavoidably touches some healthy body cells while the intent is to kill only the cancer. Such incidental contact is both unintended and unavoidable. At no time is there any desire to bring hurt to the cancer patient. Similarly, there is no punishment in godly discipline. Two thousand years ago, Christ suffered all the punishment we deserve today when Jesus was unjustly murdered as payment for the sins of humanity. Remember, correction absent any punishment consists of teaching, coaching, mentoring, and nurturing. Godly discipline is, in fact, a blessing and a joy for us to receive. It is a gift. Such correction is another reason to celebrate our relationship with God and to thank Him.

Review of Counseling Session 5

1. The Joshua Protocol prayer method is a versatile tool that can be adapted to address a variety of emotional wounds, hurts, and bad habits.
2. A healthy emotional makeup requires a balance between a person's sympathetic and parasympathetic nervous systems.
3. "Reasoning Faith" accepts the principles of science, medicine, and technology. These concepts are then combined with Christian spirituality and a belief in God. The result is a super-charged and highly effective approach to living.
4. The Joshua Protocol in brief: "It's not me. God, thank you for your forgiveness, fellowship, and discipline."

Counseling Session 6
Experiencing Change

This final therapy session was about closure. After four months, I sensed that I needed to put an end to the formal counseling process. My feeling was that I had received an extreme amount of valuable information from the Counselor, and it was now up to me to use the information to transform my life—or not. Success or failure was ultimately dependent upon me and my willingness to consistently apply the principles I had been taught. I saw no need to extend my therapy or to take any more of the Counselor's valuable time for mere "hand holding" or babysitting. The season during which I sought help from another older, wiser, person was ending. But I wanted one last session with the Counselor to wrap-up some loose ends and to answer some final questions.

The Counselor was aware that this would be our last session together. By way of an opening summary, he began the final meeting by saying: "This is material you can go over for years to come. It was a distillation of a lot of things that go on in the counseling profession, and in our Christian faith, but put in words as simple as I can make them. This is so you can try to pull some practical applications out of all this in the future."

Eric Roderiques

The Bible is But a Single Word

The Counselor then went on to talk about how Jewish rabbis say the whole of the Bible is one statement. Written into the Hebrew alphabet, the sixth letter is the connective *vav*, which can be translated "and" or "hook." The Counselor used this Hebrew letter to illustrate the interconnectedness of the Bible. He said if a person tries to prove a point or win an argument by isolating and focusing on one single piece of the Scriptures, the Bible quickly "unravels." He went on to explain that, in Acts 20:27 (ESV), the apostle Paul talked about the importance of seeking the "whole counsel" of God. In the original Greek language, the word for "counsel," *boulē* (βουλή), means "will or purpose." The Greek translation, therefore, suggests that the fullness of God's will or purpose can only be understood when we consider the Bible in its entirety.

The Counselor then, as he had earlier, invited me to think of the Bible as being symbolized and represented as a mirror that reflects and reveals to us the face of God. But just as a mirror cannot function properly if you remove a piece from the middle of it, all the stories of the Bible are similarly interwoven and function in a highly integrated fashion, almost as a single unit. The Counselor concluded by insisting that Jesus, himself, is personified and conveyed throughout the whole of the Bible, and not just in the New Testament.

The point of this discussion is to alert us to use caution as we explore biblical topics. For example, in the Gibeonite account in which Joshua and the Israelites were deceived, we would be wise to review other areas of the Bible as well, so to properly interpret the impact of the Gibeonite incident. The Counselor performed years of scholarly research covering the whole of the Bible. He did this to determine that his interpretation of the Gibeonite story, and the resultant Joshua Protocol, were both doctrinally sound. What we must never do, however, is to simply pluck easy answers to complex questions from isolated verses of the Scriptures. We are forced to become careful students of the Bible, so to build an accurate understanding of the truth that exists within the written Word. God's invitation is that we build a deep relationship with Him. How better to achieve such a personal connection than to immerse ourselves in His Word and to accurately understand God's biblical theology?

A lot of people are turned off by the idea of studying the theology of the Bible. They do not like the idea of learning about "dogmas" and ancient practices associated with a "religion." But, I have already mentioned how C.S. Lewis, in his *Mere Christianity*, compared theology to a kind of road "map" that extends our understanding of God. Let us now consider this way of thinking more fully. In his book, C.S. Lewis offers an example of a man who is walking on a beach along the Atlantic Coast. Lewis vividly describes the man's exhilarating experience of cold surf and the warm sun on his skin: The expansive vistas and the distant horizons are visually stunning, while the cries of the seagulls and the captivating roar and rumble of the turbulent, crashing waves onto the beach are stimulating to the man's auditory senses. In such a beautiful environment, he feels entirely at one with both God and nature. The experience is real in the way it stimulates, awakens, and utterly captivates the man's senses and imagination.

By the same token, if the man quickly moves indoors to look at a map of the Atlantic Coast, his experience will be very different. Rather than a multi-sensory explosion of wind, surf, and sound, the man will most likely be reduced to looking at some sort of a graphical representation of his physical location—some variety of map. The man's experience of the Atlantic Coast will instantly become less exciting to his bodily senses. But C.S. Lewis would argue the map offers a much grander understanding of the Atlantic Coast and the world beyond, as opposed to what may be learned during a stroll along a beach. "Theology is like the map," says Lewis, "If you want to get any further, you must use the map."

The Bible is a complex, comprehensive, and fully integrated single statement. It is an indispensable means by which we may achieve our goal of enjoying a better and closer relationship with God. The Counselor advises that we use the Bible as a kind of roadmap to guide and grow our knowledge and understanding of the things of heaven.

The Significance of the Joshua Protocol

Recall once again the biblical lesson from the Gibeonite deception of the Israelites, as told in the book of Joshua. Today, we are similarly seduced by the ways and values of our culture that make us focus on ourselves rather than on God. Moreover, once we have been rendered toxic by the world, Christians will only then run to God to ask Him, "What do we do now?" The answer is that God wants us to *use* our sin by symbolically burning it within the pit of sacrifice at His altar. In more practical terms, we must take our bad behaviors to the cross where Jesus died. By confessing and surrendering our bad habits to Christ, the Cross of Jesus absolves us of our unwise choices for all time. The altar of God has the ultimate power to destroy evil and to free us from its consequences. But our freedom can only be achieved through frequent and heartfelt prayer and devotion.

On Forgiveness

Some people are naturally quick to forgive the insults and injuries that come from others. If that describes you, then feel free to skip to the next section of this book. Otherwise, read on and pay close attention to what I learned during my last therapy session. It was during this tumultuous final meeting with the Counselor that he unleashed a rapid-fire and challenging monologue on the subject of forgiveness. He had done one of his doctoral dissertations on the integration of what he called "medical forgiveness" with "theological forgiveness." He told me the key to understanding the concept of forgiveness is to realize that it is a "multi-faceted package deal." *Forgiveness* must be combined with the idea of *reconciliation.* Together, these two principles culminate in the Hebrew term, *shalom*, which means peace and wholeness. A person must embrace all of these concepts to be in right standing with God. This is especially the case when it comes to addressing one's own enemies, and those who have hurt us. The Counselor began by saying that, ultimately, God alone has the right to forgive people. Our job is to agree with this divine source of forgiveness and to be in full accord when God forgives our enemies.

Again, the Counselor argued that the choice to forgive is not really ours, but only reconciliation is fully under human control. Consider how the words *forgiveness* and *reconciliation* are often defined. *Forgiveness* is a powerful word that can mean to "pardon" somebody for an offense. Such a pardon is a total grant of absolution, as would be required to remedy a miscarriage of justice or to remove the stigma of a criminal law conviction made against a person. By comparison, the word *reconciliation* is a more muted term and can mean to restore civility to a tense situation and to engage in fence-mending for the purpose of normalizing relationships.[103] In this sense, reconciliation seems to be a less perfect outcome in the aftermath of a conflict, but it remains a way for people and society to move forward again with life after some kind of disruptive trauma or dispute has taken place.

Sometimes we utter words like, "I can't forgive him" or "I'll never forgive them!" But these are nonsense statements, as God alone has the power to pardon. We must undergo a change in our thinking. We need to understand that, when God forgives our enemy, their "old and sinful self" is destroyed in His eyes, and a new person in eternity (i.e., in heaven) emerges. This approach seems very peculiar until you understand that God has a different way of looking at the concept of time. God views individuals who are dysfunctional in today's world, as if they were already perfected and fully restored and living in the heaven God intends for their future. For God, that perfected future has already arrived. This weird view of time, place, and circumstances opens the door for us to reconcile with the people who hurt us. Once reconciliation takes place, then we can find inner peace and live our lives in *shalom*.

But is this way of thinking just a bunch of childish and wishful pretense and make-believe? What about people who suffer egregious acts of violence and are hurt at the hands of others? How can forgiveness, reconciliation, and *shalom* take place when there are terrifying circumstances such as rape, incest, torture, or criminal violence? How can people be expected to reconcile with such evil? The answer is that we should seek restoration immediately, not from our heads (which are filled with our own problems and dysfunctions) but from our hearts. In Matthew 18:35, Jesus talks about how true forgiveness comes from our "hearts," or more literally, from our spiritual core faith in God. Remember, we do not control forgiveness. God is the real source of all forgiveness. Our task is to get into agreement with Him, as *the Lord forgives* our enemies.

With Christ's death upon the cross, God has chosen the path of forgiveness for us, and we should do the same for others. However, a problem exists in how the lower primal brain is contaminated with the world's desire for anger, hatred, and revenge. Therefore, we must forgive out of a sincere and determined obedience to God. This is a key point. The emphasis here is on our cooperation with the greater will of God, because our hearts may find it difficult to forgive a tremendous evil that was done to us. But the Counselor says, in such instances, we must fall upon our faces in raw obedience to God. It is as if to say, "Okay, God, I believe you have forgiven this other person for the horrible things they did to hurt me, and I am not going to dispute your decision to absolve them of their guilt. I respect *you*, Lord, and I am not going to become angry with you for forgiving my enemy. You acquitted them of their terrible acts, just as you have forgiven me for my many transgressions. You have exonerated them—and I am okay with it."

To make it clearer, imagine your best friend announces he is going to marry someone who you know is a bad person. And after you gently share your concerns, he chooses to go ahead with his wedding plans anyway. At that point, you must make a choice: either run the risk of losing your best friend or accept his decision. Similarly, we must support the decision of God to forgive our worst enemy. If we choose not to, it will only hinder our relationship with the Lord. God lives within us. We are the body of Christ with the Holy Spirit existing inside of us. We are defined, not by a visceral lower-brain, but by the mind of an upper-brain that houses our spirit-consciousness. The Holy Spirit is expressed within us, and it becomes a matter of our primal brain gradually agreeing (this takes a span of time) with the greater will of God. Often, we may need to work at accepting God's decision to forgive our enemy. Bible teacher Joyce Meyer talks about how sometimes forgiveness does not just happen quickly and easily but becomes a process. She says when it is hard for us to pardon others, we need to be "willing to be willing" to forgive what was done to hurt us. Growth and maturity often come in baby steps.

Attempt Reconciliation

After acknowledging and accepting God's decision to pardon another person's sin that hurt us, we should ourselves seek reconciliation with the other person. The New Testament Bible addresses the importance of reconciliation in Matthew 18:15. Again, to *reconcile* with somebody who hurt you means to rebuild or re-create some type of ongoing and healthier relationship with that person. This may not always be possible, especially if the other person is dangerous or unwilling to normalize their behaviors and actions towards you. *The Counselor warns that great caution must be taken not to place ourselves in jeopardy when reconciling with another person*. But barring such extremes, best efforts should be made to re-establish relations with the person who caused us injury.

Perhaps one of the best examples of large-scale reconciliation took place in the nation of South Africa in the 1990s, after the era of apartheid ended. *Apartheid* was a South African system of racial segregation that had existed for decades until it was finally over-turned at the end of the twentieth century. Once the black majority assumed political control in South Africa, a "South African Truth and Reconciliation Commission" was established. The Commission traveled across South Africa in a series of public hearings to discuss the horrendous acts of violence and discrimination that were the legacy of apartheid.

The reconciliation that took place in South Africa was extreme and unusual. It may not be possible for individuals to find it within themselves to so wholly set aside the hurts of the past. But keep in mind that there can be different levels of reconciliation. While you might never experience feelings of warmth and friendliness towards your past enemy, you can perhaps learn to show them civility and politeness—as you would to a stranger. Better to treat a former abuser like a stranger, than as a hated enemy. If you can achieve reconciliation, you will be the one who ultimately benefits the most from the effort. By attaining reconciliation and closure with your past, you will find an inner peace for your future.

Achieving Shalom

As we have said earlier, *shalom* (שָׁלוֹם) is the Hebrew word meaning *peace* and wholeness. We achieve inner peace through our faith in the perfect will of God. We can have no peace without being in right standing and agreement with the Lord. If our emotions balk at the notion of forgiveness and reconciliation, then we must lean on our belief in God as the supreme arbiter. As we have already discussed, God is the ultimate dispenser of forgiveness. God's grace and mercy towards our enemies trumps our own anger, bitterness, and hatred.

If through our higher-level consciousness we can override the angry feelings of a lower primal brain, then we can enjoy a victory and celebrate in *shalom*. The prize to be had is what the Bible calls *perfect peace*.[104] But such peace comes at the cost of crucifying and subduing the flesh. We must fight for dominance and control of our thoughts and behaviors. Once we gain such self-control, then we can reasonably say that we have attained a level of spiritual maturity. Self-control is demonstrated when we consistently deny our negative emotions and habits, and instead transform our sins into godly worship. By embracing a Christian faith capable of taking your sins to the cross, God can put you into *shalom*.

Transformation is All About Taking Control

We fall victim to fate and determinism when we do not believe in the concept of free will, and then fail to exercise our capacity to choose our own proper course of action. The Counselor was adamant that there is such a thing as free will and that a person can use the power of the mind to choose his or her own path in life. Only when we abandon our ability to choose, do we become (by default) dominated by a lower primal brain, by society, by our environment, and potentially by any unseen spiritual forces that may be warring against us. It is essential to emphasize a higher consciousness, separate and independent from the physical realm, so that we can experience change agency—or transformation. Consider what the Bible says about the idea of transformation. The apostle Paul, in Romans 12:2 (NIV), stated it plainly:

> Do not conform to the pattern of this world, but
> be transformed by the renewing of your mind.

Throughout this book, the notion of transformation has been a key theme. The word Paul used to describe the idea of transformation, is translated into the Greek as *metamorphosis*.[105]

Metamorphosis means to change. When we pray, and when we use the approach to prayer suggested by the Joshua Protocol, we are resisting domination by the lower brain. Moreover, we must simultaneously exercise the power of the upper brain and force our higher self to become strong and in control. In Matthew 11:12 (ESV), the Bible says the kingdom of heaven suffers violence, and the violent take it by force. We can interpret this Scripture to mean that if we want to get better, it will require some effort on our part. Hard effort. Each of us must vigorously assert our real self upon our socially-conditioned self. The primal brain, in many ways, acts like a separate organism operating within the body. But when we hit it with aggression or strong emotion, coming from the upper brain, the lower brain becomes submissive and compliant.[106] The mind can give the lower primal brain instructions and commands, and the lower brain will ultimately obey—if we are consistent and forceful in the way we train it.

By contrast, if we behave submissively and allow the lower brain to dominate the mind, then the results can be disastrous in the way our primal instincts will absorb the totality of our being. If we timidly say to ourselves, "Oh, I am so sorry that I had a bad thought, but I can't help myself." Or, if we sheepishly think, "I cannot believe I did such a bad thing, but I'll never change"—we open the door and will be consumed by a primal brain that only responds to strength. The correct approach is the one we already discussed involving the Joshua Protocol. We must always respond quickly to any mental or emotional negativity that arises from within us. We must state emphatically: *"It's not me!"* followed by the three-step prayer process that instantaneously transforms sin into godly worship. The entire response takes only a few seconds, and is easy to recite, whether done silently or aloud:

> It's not me.
> God, thank you for your forgiveness.

> God, thank you for your fellowship.
> God, thank you for your discipline.

Moreover, now that you have read this book, you have a much better appreciation for both the neuroscience and the biblical foundations that support the Joshua Protocol. Given your increased level of understanding, you can afford to further simplify the Protocol into a pair of short sentences that quickly and easily roll off the tongue:

> It's not me. God, thank you for your forgiveness, fellowship, and discipline.

Some people have told me that all of this discussion seems too good to be true. But in fact, for many years, the Counselor has successfully tested this approach to behavior modification within his therapy practice, and many of his clients have enjoyed substantial healing. My own life experience has proven to me that this system really works. A simple, positive, and consistent testimony before God can result in a subdued and domesticated lower brain. Through *repeated* and consistent application of the Joshua Protocol, we can bring our primal instincts into captivity and put our lower natures under the control of the mind. We can invoke the power of the creator of the universe and defeat Satan's plan for our destruction. God will cite our genuine, unfailing, and heartfelt thank messages to Him as the inducement He requires before making hell tremble and flee from us.

Pray for Others

Lastly, think about adding one final step to the Joshua Protocol. If you have hurt someone (as I did through my interactions with the young boy, Bobby) or if someone has hurt you (such as I experienced in the story of A) pray for the other person. Clearly, we should petition God to restore those whom we have injured, but we also should appeal to God on behalf of those who injure *us*. On the surface, this last statement seems foolish. Why pray blessings for our abusers, enemies, or tempters?

The answer lies in the instructions Christians received from Jesus during his Sermon on the Mount:

> But I tell you, love your enemies and pray for those who persecute you.[107]

It is much easier to pray for those we have hurt, whether our actions against them were intentional or accidental. The more significant challenge is to pray for those who have hurt or tempted us. For example, if I am out in a public setting, and casually encounter some foolish young woman who is inappropriately dressed, I can use the Joshua Protocol to fend-off any wrong thinking on my part. But I can also add a short prayer that is designed to help the young woman. I can ask God to change how she views herself. I can petition the Lord to render her more mature and to better value and understand her worth. Moreover, I can pray that the young woman is respected and cherished by society, even though she is presenting herself to the world in a way that makes her look more like a prostitute than a much-beloved daughter of God. My simple prayer might be something like this:

> It's not me. God, thank you for your forgiveness, fellowship, and discipline. *And God bless her.*

The addition of "God bless her" is a suitable intercessory prayer that seeks the Lord's favor for the inappropriately-dressed young woman.

Similarly, if I am about my regular daily business, but suddenly experience someone or something that triggers a wounded or angry emotional response in me, I should quickly use the Joshua Protocol to wrestle my thoughts back onto a healthier path.[108] In other words, as soon as I become mindfully aware that my emotions and brain have been hijacked and are moving in a wrong or dangerous direction, I should act to prayerfully rebuke those wrong thoughts and feelings. I must immediately fight to get my own emotional house in order. If a person offends me, I can also pray a short prayer for my foe, so that God can help him or her to change, grow, and improve. I can pray that God should bless them to become healthier in their relationships with other people. For example:

> It's not me. God, thank you for your forgiveness, fellowship, and discipline. *And God bless them.*

Allow me to be clear here. I am not saying that you should pray for an adversary's financial prosperity or career advancement or other material gain, but instead pray for their improved mental and emotional wholeness and normalcy.

Story of The Little Red Lizard

Of course, some people will simply dismiss the whole idea of the Joshua Protocol as impractical. Such individuals will reason something like the following: "I can't be praying all day long! I've got work to do and many other responsibilities. My brain frequently moves in wrong directions, with all kinds of inappropriate thoughts, feelings, fantasies, cravings, desires, and the like. I can't help it. I would need to use the Joshua Protocol many times each day. That's just not reasonable; I'm too busy. It's a losing battle."

I find it interesting how some of us are willing to entertain bad, harmful, and even dangerous thoughts all day long, but if challenged to instead pray, we think prayer requires too much effort. The Bible tells us we should be in constant prayer. The apostle Paul urges us to "pray without ceasing."[109] But people make excuses, and self-deception happens. Many in society fail to confront the difficult and painful choices of life. To put it briefly, we often run away from our problems because we fear the trials of life will be too hurtful or too hard to conquer. C.S. Lewis, in *The Great Divorce*, tells a story about how individuals will often choose hell over heaven, simply because hell offers the path of least resistance. Lewis describes one episode involving a conversation between a heavenly angel and a "Ghost." The Ghost was a deceased human being whose immortal spirit had to make a choice between spending eternity in heaven or in hell. The problem was that the Ghost still carried with him an addiction to lust, which had become an obstacle to his achieving heaven.

C.S. Lewis made the sin of lust more concrete for his readers by symbolizing it in the form of a "little red lizard." In Lewis' story, the lusty little red lizard perched itself atop the shoulder of the hapless Ghost, and continuously tormented the Ghost by whispering the lizard's evil and seductive suggestions. Ashamed and disheartened, the Ghost was ready to forever give up any hope of heaven, and instead voluntarily retreat to hell. But, at the last moment, an angel appeared and offered to help the Ghost—by destroying the little red lizard. The following short abstract captures the tone and summarizes the underlying message found in C.S. Lewis' famous original work.

THE GHOST: "But *killing* him seems drastic."

THE ANGEL: "Give me your permission to kill the little red lizard."

THE GHOST: "Get back! You're burning me. How can I tell you to kill the little red lizard? You'd kill *me* too."

THE ANGEL:	"That is not true."
THE GHOST:	"But, you're already hurting me now."
THE ANGEL:	"I never said killing the little red lizard wouldn't *hurt* you. I just said it wouldn't *kill* you."

The decision to become healthier and to stop making bad choices requires some short-term pain and discomfort when we finally make an effort to forgo our bad habits. Such temporary inconvenience and hurt is the price that people must pay to secure long-term freedom and happiness.

Your future is at stake. How reasonable is it to allow your lower brain to continue to cause chaos in your life? Your lower brain is like the little red lizard. While you may not struggle with the sin of lust, you should not allow other destructive patterns or "garbage thinking" to define you. Is it really "easier" to passively continue to live with those damaging behavioral patterns that have long caused you such grief, upset, and regret, and which have compelled you to seek answers and solutions from this book? Consistently using the Joshua Protocol, and building a close personal relationship with God using prayer and meditation, is the right approach for anyone who is serious about becoming mentally and emotionally healthier and happier.

The Counselor went on to tell me that God wants to perfect us from "the inside out." God is not interested in any surface aesthetics, or any superficial religiosity on our part. Imagine washing only the outside of a dirty coffee cup. Who would want to drink from a cup that is filthy on the inside, and has had only its exterior washed and sanitized? In Matthew 23:27 (ESV), Jesus complained that the Pharisees were like whitewashed tombs over dead men's bones. He said, "Woe to you, scribes and Pharisees, hypocrites! For you are like whitewashed tombs, which outwardly appear beautiful, but within are full of dead people's bones and all uncleanness." God is interested in transforming us at the level of our core being. In the Scriptures, He talks about "changing men's hearts."[110] Such manner of speaking expresses the hope of profoundly growing our inner spirituality, and of reshaping our identity to more closely resemble that of Jesus. The *heart*, as described in the Bible, is the spiritual core of a person. It is the part of us that only God fully sees. Our main purpose in life is to cooperate and to allow our Lord to use the challenges of this worldly existence to fundamentally change us. God seeks to transform and reshape our spiritual core so that it more closely resembles Jesus Christ, who serves as a role model for humanity.

Is Change Happening in Me?

If you choose to adopt the ideas and practices outlined in this book, how will you know whether these concepts are working to improve your life? How can you tell if you are becoming a healthier, better person, and are becoming free of your old bad habits, lousy choices, or negative attitudes? For an answer, consider the biblical story of Joseph and Potiphar's wife. Genesis 39 (NIV) tells of how Joseph was a handsome young Jewish man who worked for a wealthy and powerful official of the Egyptian Pharaoh. This high-ranking Egyptian leader was named Potiphar. Moreover, we learn from the biblical text that Potiphar had a wife who held a predatory sexual interest in young Joseph. Verses 11 and 12 set the scene for her attempt at seduction:

> One day he [Joseph] went into [Potiphar's] house to attend to his duties, and none of the household servants was inside. She caught him by his cloak and said, "Come to bed with me!" But he left his cloak in her hand and ran out of the house.

We can guess that Potiphar's wife was young, attractive, and served as something of a trophy bride for her influential husband. Given the circumstances, Joseph may well have felt some physical temptation to enter into an adulterous affair with such a desirable and sexually eager woman. Yet, the Scripture says Joseph fled the opportunity to behave inappropriately.

The lesson here deals with how healthy people react when they are confronted with chances to do wrong, unwise, or even dangerous things. Ultimately, such people turn away from opportunities to sin. Success depends upon whether you embrace a lifestyle that includes regular prayer, meditation, and biblical study. If you consistently fight wrong thinking and dysfunctional impulses by using the Joshua Protocol, then the long process of reshaping your brain through neuroplasticity should begin quickly. I, myself, started to see some real and positive changes happening in my life within the first few months.

The desired healing and transformation require at least one or two years of consistent application of the principles taught in this text. But as your brain grows healthier and your old habits and negative responses start to fade, you will increasingly find that you are emotionally *repulsed* whenever society or life presents you with new opportunities to engage in things that are destructive or unwholesome. The feeling of being sickened or repelled each time you are exposed to toxic external influences will be a clue that you are in the process of growing healthier.

Consider, as an example, a man who is in recovery from pornography addiction. If such a man is casually surfing the Internet and innocently stumbles onto a web page that contains an inappropriate photograph, his old inclination would be to immediately engage and start fantasizing and consuming the pornographic image he sees. But upon undergoing the process of brain change, that same man who later stumbles upon an obscene Internet photo will be made to feel uneasy by it. He will promptly move to another web page or just walk away, altogether. The healthy man's new instinctive reflex will be to somehow escape from the source of any temptation—much in the same way Joseph fled the temptation of Potiphar's pretty wife.

Threat of Relapse

I had an interesting experience that began about eleven months into my recovery process. I was doing well in maintaining my thought life, integrity, and sexual purity. But then, for some unexplained reason, I became lazy and sloppy when it came to using the Joshua Protocol. I got to thinking that I was so advanced in leveraging the technique that I could afford to delay using it when inappropriate thoughts first crept into my lower brain. "It was no big deal," I rationalized. I then told myself it would be safe for me to enjoy those thoughts, "just for a little while." My twisted thinking was akin to a recovering alcoholic convincing himself that, "Just one drink will be okay." Additionally, I noticed that the frequency of these new thought attacks seemed to be on the increase. I became alarmed by the unexpected changes and began to pray for an answer.

Shortly after that, I remembered the book of Daniel from the Bible's Old Testament. Daniel became famous as a prophetic interpreter of dreams, and he experienced supernatural visions that allowed him to predict the future. In chapter 10, Daniel received his greatest vision from God, but was at first unable to interpret and understand the message. Frustrated, Daniel began a lengthy period of prayer and fasting, and it seemed like God was silent to Daniel's request for a correct interpretation of the vision God gave him. But then, weeks later, an angel with "eyes like flaming torches" appeared before Daniel. In Daniel 10:13, the angel spoke:

> Your prayer was heard, and I set out to come to you. But I was waylaid by the angel-prince of the

kingdom of Persia and was delayed for a good three weeks. But then Michael, one of the chief angel-princes, intervened to help me. I left him there with the prince of the kingdom of Persia. And now I'm here to help you understand.[111]

When you start to make real progress in your efforts to improve your life, your success may trigger increased supernatural opposition against you. For example, in the above passage, the Bible tells of how a super-demon named "the prince of the kingdom of Persia," was deployed by the underworld in an unsuccessful effort to stop Daniel from realizing his greatest achievement. Similarly, as you begin to grow and start making better life-choices, Satan may intensify his efforts and try to rob you of your victory. The devil does not want you to get healthier and to become more successful in your life. Out of desperation, hell may resort to using increasingly powerful, sophisticated, or subtler forms of spiritual warfare against you.

The battle for control over your brain will not end in your lifetime. Satan will periodically test you to see if he can make you stumble. But do not despair; such tests will become fewer as you continually grow stronger. Your ongoing success over time depends upon your constant alertness and vigilance. Simply know that you may occasionally be challenged. Be prepared to respond immediately should attacks happen. In the years ahead, consider reviewing the contents of this book, as needed, and refreshing your commitment to using these lessons. The Bible warns that, "The thief comes only to steal and kill and destroy."[112] The devil will attempt to distract or otherwise make you *forget* what you have learned from this book. After experiencing success, you may inexplicably stop using the Joshua Protocol, and not even know why. In any event, if in the future you make some mistakes or poor choices, be sure to restart your recovery program as soon as possible. Lastly, try to consider any unwanted demonic attention as a peculiar "badge of honor" that you have earned. Know that you are making real progress towards becoming a happier and healthier person. Know that God is pleased with your efforts.

Review of Counseling Session 6

1. The Bible is a highly-integrated document that must be studied, in its entirety, so to be adequately understood and correctly applied.
2. There is a fundamental difference between forgiveness and reconciliation. Ultimately, God alone has the power to forgive sins, as He is the final judge and source of mercy in the universe. It is our task to accept God's forgiveness of our enemies and to strive to achieve reconciliation with them—but only if such reconciliation can be accomplished safely. We must never put ourselves in danger when attempting to address areas of conflict with another person.
3. If we are ultimately able to reconcile with those who hurt us, then we can enter a state of greater peace and wholeness. The Hebrew word for peace and wholeness is *shalom*.
4. Brain transformation requires hard and consistent effort over an extended period of time. It also requires ongoing maintenance, so we do not slip back into our old, harmful habits.
5. Our goal should be to have our personalities and actions governed by a more virtuous upper brain, rather than by a lower brain that is driven by primal, instinctual, and animalistic urges.
6. As a person grows and matures spiritually, he or she will discover that they are increasingly repelled when confronted by toxic situations and choices. This process of character development is an ongoing one that will yield benefits as a person continues their spiritual journey through life.

Conclusion

A Better Tomorrow

The Counselor shared some of his biblical interpretations and offered his personal thoughts regarding the future of humanity. He told me we can now only see pale shadows of who we will be after the Second Coming of Christ. When Jesus returns to the earth in the future, those who believe in and follow him will be given new and perfect spiritual bodies.[113] Moreover, I was told our spirit is made of a different fabric or substance than the rest of the physical universe. The Counselor described this special fabric using a term with which I was unfamiliar. He called it "emerging conscious properties." He went on to say this material is very distinct from the substance of our mortal bodies, which he described as "emerging physical properties."[114] The main point is that our spirits will live on forever, while our bodies will one-day die. The Counselor concluded by saying the whole universe is like a huge amniotic sac, or as he called it, "the womb of heaven." His opinion is that the cosmos is giving birth to God's children, after which time the existing physical creation will make way for a new spiritual heaven and earth.

In my final minutes with the Counselor, he sought to sum up the ideas and principles taken from our prior months of discussion. He ended our counseling relationship by sharing some of his feelings and concerns. He told me:

I'm kind of happy to have been God's messenger, and to have helped you and given you a good nomenclature and superstructure to think about mind over the lower brain, and about the relationship between mind and the religious spirit. We have talked about how our Christian faith correlates, in a practical way, to the whole spectrum of life, whether it's temporal or eternal. Our faith gives us hope and gives us joy in the midst of the struggle. But the task now is one that is agreed upon by much of the helping professions, the counseling profession, and Christianity. Namely, we must apply ourselves to win the battle of mind over brain. This important challenge represents a brand-new paradigm, and it is a challenge that humanity would be wise to take seriously and to consider carefully.

As for me, I would like to end this book by restating a primary lesson I learned from the Counselor. By my way of thinking, even more essential than the important brain physiology and science that supports the concept of neuroplasticity, is the biblical idea of *transforming* sin into something else. All my life, I had been helpless against Satan, demons, the environment, our society, my lower brain—or whatever else we can finally agree was the cause of my anger, inappropriate thoughts, and other emotional imperfections and dysfunctions. In my imagination, I can now see a sorry picture of my former self with hands tied tightly behind my back. For over forty years, I had taken a relentless and merciless beating from unseen forces that I had never understood. But suddenly my hands have been set free. Today, it is something more than just being able to defend myself; now I can go on the offensive and *attack* the root cause of any problems and chase away any invisible enemies that might seek to engage me, either now or in the future.

I am again reminded of C.S. Lewis and his fantasy, *The Screwtape Letters*. At the end of that story a human being, whom an apprentice demon had targeted for damnation to hell, instead went to heaven. In the account, we catch a glimpse of how it might be possible for us in our humanity to strike a blow against evil spiritual forces that want to hurt us. The following depiction is loosely adapted from C.S. Lewis' brilliant and challenging work. But I think this simplified rendering better serves to show how our spiritual enemies might be vulnerable. In the following portrayal, the master demon, named Screwtape, recounts to a lesser demon what happened to their human prey who unexpectedly escaped to heaven and was united with God:

> Did you notice how naturally the earth-born insect entered the new life? How all of the man's doubts and fears became, in the twinkling of an eye, ridiculous? As he saw you, he also saw *Them*, the angels. I know how it was. You reeled back dizzy and blinded, more hurt by the presence of angels than the man by death. The degradation of it! The fact that this thing of earth and slime could stand upright and talk with spirits before whom you, yourself a spirit, could only cower. He saw not only *Them*, but he saw *Him*... God. This animal, this thing conceived in a bed, could suddenly look upon *God*. What is blinding, suffocating fire to you, is now cool and refreshing light to the man.

C.S. Lewis suggests that our closeness and right standing with God causes discomfort to any evil spiritual forces that may lurk nearby. Much in the same way, the Counselor would argue that when our thought processes go awry, due to demonic influence or some other natural interference by our primal brains, we can promptly respond with powerful and prayerful "thank messages" to God. Our prayerfulness and worship brings us spiritually closer in relationship to our creator and helps us normalize our thinking patterns.

The Defeat of Evil

Interestingly, when our personal relationship with God deepens, C.S. Lewis proposes that we avail ourselves of an effective kind of spiritual energy that is experienced as pain by any nearby evil and invisible adversaries. From Lewis' work, we can infer that prayer must somehow cause our evil occult enemies to become "dizzy, blinded, and hurt." Prayer to God forces wicked spirits and devils to literally "cower, suffocate," and ultimately to "reel" and flee from us. Moreover, the pain we inflict through our prayerful spiritual warfare may discourage demonic forces from bothering us in the future. Once we are free from adverse spiritual influences, we can start to live life in a new and exciting way. This idea of fighting back against the world's negativity gives me great encouragement and hope for the future. It should give you greater confidence, too.

I just love it. I love the fantastic news that God can use someone like me to help Him turn-the-tables on the devil, and to help advance God's agenda of defeating evil in this world.[115] Whenever Satan ambushes me by injecting an inappropriate thought into my primal brain, I have the Joshua Protocol as a quick and ready tool for unleashing spiritual violence against my evil enemy. Additionally, my journey in recovery has made me a better student of the Bible; I am one who continues to practice and improve in the arts of prayer and meditation. Although I am far from perfect, I can report an enhanced inner peace that comes as I continue to invest and grow in my friendship with the creator of the universe.

Lastly, through these pages, I hope I have successfully communicated the idea that it is fruitless to resist evil. We are all challenged, broken, or perhaps have made some poor life choices.

Only Jesus Christ knew no sin and was perfect. We cannot hope to overcome our negative thinking, bad attitudes, and hurtful addictions by trying to be "good enough" or "strong enough" or through any sort of human "willpower." Our best option is to ask God to transform the bad in us and to change it into something good. We must seek to transform evil by consuming it as a kind of fuel that propels us closer to God and makes us stronger in both our minds and emotions. Stop resisting sin, and start transforming it. Improve your life by developing a growing and ever-closer personal relationship with God.

Review of the Conclusion

1. The Counselor told me that the physical universe is a kind of temporary incubator that God is using to grow and mature His spiritual children. Ultimately, God's children are destined to live with Him in heaven.
2. It is possible to transform our bad behaviors into something more positive. With God's help, we can change any evil thoughts or urges we might experience.
3. Spiritual warfare is a real and ongoing phenomenon. It affects and shapes the lives of everyday people.
4. By using the tools discussed in this book, such as the Joshua Protocol, it is possible for us to wage successful spiritual warfare. Rather than being passive victims, we can now use prayer to aggressively attack any unseen spiritual adversaries that oppose us.
5. Ultimately, to change a person's bad habits is less a matter of human willpower and more about seeking a close personal relationship with God. Such a spiritual connection with the creator of the universe can unleash massive healing and transformational power that will improve the life of anyone who earnestly seeks to know God.

Appendix 1
Additional Applications

The following shows several examples of how the Joshua Protocol prayer method may be adapted to address a variety of circumstances and emotional needs. For each of the following situations, pray in the manner outlined *every time* you have a negative, inappropriate, or dysfunctional thought or feeling. Even if you need to pray one of the following prayers, dozens of times per day, for many months—do so. It is okay to make small adjustments to the language, so to best meet your needs. Whether you say the prayers audibly or silently in your mind does not matter. What *does* matter is that you use consistency when battling negative thoughts and emotions; this is essential to success in changing your bad habits. As you become accustomed to using prayer as a spiritual weapon, you will likely see the frequency of your negative thinking and feelings start to decline over time. Moreover, when you become mentally and emotionally healthier, the process of healing will become more natural as your confidence in the process grows.

Once you become more accustomed to using the Joshua Protocol, you will be able to shorten your prayers, and they will still carry weight and hold meaning and power for you. Ultimately, the Joshua Protocol can be briefly summarized as follows:

> It's not me. God, thank you for your forgiveness, fellowship, and discipline.

But at the start of your recovery program, consider meditating on the full prayer. Here are some examples for you to think about. Feel free to develop similar thought tools on your own, using the following format:

The Joshua Protocol for Obsessive-Compulsive Disorder (OCD)

Step 1: It's not me, it's just my OCD.

Step 2: God, thank you for your forgiveness, in case I have made any mistakes in how I have dealt with (or failed to address) my OCD.

Step 3: God, thank you for your fellowship; I am not alone in this fight against my OCD. Your Holy Spirit indwells me and strengthens me. I need have no fear in this area. Fear is not of God.

Step 4: God, thank you for your perfect discipline. Godly discipline is without punishment, blame, or shame; it is a blessing whereby God teaches, coaches, and encourages me as I prayerfully overcome my OCD in the name of Jesus Christ, and through the power of the Holy Spirit.

The Joshua Protocol for Overcoming Low Self-Esteem

Step 1: It's not me, it's just my low self-esteem.

Step 2: God, thank you for your forgiveness, in case I have made any mistakes in the way I have dealt with (or failed to address) my low self-esteem.

Step 3: God, thank you for your fellowship; I am not alone in this fight against low self-esteem. Your Holy Spirit indwells me and strengthens me. I need have no fear in this area. Fear is not of God.

Step 4: God, thank you for your perfect discipline. Godly discipline is without punishment, blame, or shame; it is a blessing whereby God teaches, coaches, and encourages me as I prayerfully overcome low self-esteem, in the name of Jesus Christ and through the power of the Holy Spirit.

The Joshua Protocol for Overcoming a Poor Attitude

Step 1: It's not me, it's just my poor attitude.

Step 2: God, thank you for your forgiveness, in case I have made any mistakes in how I have dealt with (or failed to address) my poor attitude.

Step 3: God, thank you for your fellowship; I am not alone in this fight against a poor attitude. Your Holy Spirit indwells me and strengthens me. I need have no fear in this area. Fear is not of God.

Step 4: God, thank you for your perfect discipline. Godly discipline is without punishment, blame, or shame; it is a blessing whereby God teaches, coaches, and encourages me as I prayerfully overcome a poor attitude in the name of Jesus Christ, and through the power of the Holy Spirit.

The Joshua Protocol for Overcoming Laziness

Step 1: It's not me, it's just my laziness.

Step 2: God, thank you for your forgiveness, in case I have made any mistakes in how I have dealt with (or failed to address) my lazy ways.

Step 3: God, thank you for your fellowship; I am not alone in this fight against laziness. Your Holy Spirit indwells me and strengthens me. I need have no fear in this area. Fear is not of God.

Step 4: God, thank you for your perfect discipline. Godly discipline is without punishment, blame, or shame; it is a blessing whereby God teaches, coaches, and encourages me as I prayerfully overcome my lazy tendencies, in the name of Jesus Christ, and through the power of the Holy Spirit.

The Joshua Protocol for Overcoming Procrastination

Step 1: It's not me, it's just my problem of putting certain things off.

Step 2: God, thank you for your forgiveness, in case I have made any mistakes in how I have dealt with (or failed to address) procrastination.

Step 3: God, thank you for your fellowship; I am not alone in this fight against procrastination. Your Holy Spirit indwells me and strengthens me. I need have no fear in this area. Fear is not of God.

Step 4: God, thank you for your perfect discipline. Godly discipline is without punishment, blame, or shame; it is a blessing whereby God teaches, coaches, and encourages me as I prayerfully overcome my tendency to postpone specific tasks. I pray this healing prayer in the name of Jesus Christ, and through the power of the Holy Spirit.

The Joshua Protocol for Overcoming Gossip

Step 1: It's not me, it's just my bad habit of gossiping.

Step 2: God, thank you for your forgiveness, in case I have made any mistakes in how I have dealt with (or failed to address) my loose mouth.

Step 3: God, thank you for your fellowship; I am not alone in my fight against idle talking. Your Holy Spirit indwells me and strengthens me. I need have no fear in this area. Fear is not of God.

Step 4: God, thank you for your perfect discipline. Godly discipline is without punishment, blame, or shame; it is a blessing whereby God teaches, coaches, and encourages me as I prayerfully overcome my gossipy tendencies, in the name of Jesus Christ, and through the power of the Holy Spirit.

The Joshua Protocol for Overcoming Sadness

Step 1: It's not me, it's just my feelings of sadness.

Step 2: God, thank you for your forgiveness, in case I have made any mistakes in the way I have dealt with (or failed to address) my sad emotions.

Step 3: God, thank you for your fellowship; I am not alone in this fight against sadness. Your Holy Spirit indwells me and strengthens me. I need have no fear in this area. Fear is not of God.

Step 4: God, thank you for your perfect discipline. Godly discipline is without punishment, blame, or shame; it is a blessing whereby God teaches, coaches, and encourages me as I prayerfully overcome feelings of sadness in the name of Jesus Christ, and through the power of the Holy Spirit.

The Joshua Protocol for Stealing

Step 1: It's not me, it's just my dysfunctional desire to steal things.

Step 2: God, thank you for your forgiveness, in case I have made any mistakes in how I have dealt with (or failed to address) my emotional need to take what does not belong to me.

Step 3: God, thank you for your fellowship; I am not alone in this fight against habitual stealing. Your Holy Spirit indwells me and strengthens me. I need have no fear in this area. Fear is not of God.

Step 4: God, thank you for your perfect discipline. Godly discipline is without punishment, blame, or shame; it is a blessing whereby God teaches, coaches, and encourages me as I prayerfully overcome my compulsions, in the name of Jesus Christ, and through the power of the Holy Spirit.

The Joshua Protocol for Liars

Step 1: It's not me, it's just my unhealthy habit of telling lies to others.

Step 2: God, thank you for your forgiveness, in case I have made any mistakes in how I have dealt with (or failed to address) my chronic untruthfulness.

Step 3: God, thank you for your fellowship; I am not alone in this fight against habitual lying. Your Holy Spirit indwells me and strengthens me. I need have no fear in this area. Fear is not of God.

Step 4: God, thank you for your perfect discipline. Godly discipline is without punishment, blame, or shame; it is a blessing whereby God teaches, coaches, and encourages me as I prayerfully commit to telling the truth, in the name of Jesus Christ, and through the power of the Holy Spirit.

The Joshua Protocol for Post-Traumatic Stress Disorder (PTSD)

Step 1: It's not me, it's just my PTSD.

Step 2: God, thank you for your forgiveness, in case I have made any mistakes in the way I have dealt with (or failed to address) my PTSD.

Step 3: God, thank you for your fellowship; I am not alone in this fight against my PTSD. Your Holy Spirit indwells me and strengthens me. I need have no fear in this area. Fear is not of God.

Step 4: God, thank you for your perfect discipline. Godly discipline is without punishment, blame, or shame; it is a blessing whereby God teaches, coaches, and encourages me as I prayerfully overcome my PTSD in the name of Jesus Christ, and through the power of the Holy Spirit.

The Joshua Protocol for Excessive Preoccupation with Entertainment

Step 1: It's not me, it's just my preoccupation with entertainment.

Step 2: God, thank you for your forgiveness, in case I have made any mistakes in how I have dealt with (or failed to address) my preoccupation with entertainment.

Step 3: God, thank you for your fellowship; I am not alone in this fight against my preoccupation with entertainment. Your Holy Spirit indwells me and strengthens me. I need have no fear in this area. Fear is not of God.

Step 4: God, thank you for your perfect discipline. Godly discipline is without punishment, blame, or shame; it is a blessing whereby God teaches, coaches, and encourages me as I prayerfully overcome my preoccupation with entertainment, in the name of Jesus Christ and through the power of the Holy Spirit.

The Joshua Protocol for Unwarranted Fear and Anxiety

Step 1: It's not me, it's just my unwarranted fear and anxiety.

Step 2: God, thank you for your forgiveness, in case I have made any mistakes in the way I have dealt with (or failed to address) my irrational fear and anxiety.

Step 3: God, thank you for your fellowship; I am not alone in this fight against fear and anxiety. Your Holy Spirit indwells me and strengthens me. I need have no concern or doubt in this area. Fear and anxiety are not of God.

Step 4: God, thank you for your perfect discipline. Godly discipline is without punishment, blame, or shame; it is a blessing whereby God teaches, coaches, and encourages me as I prayerfully overcome my unnecessary fear and anxiety in the name of Jesus Christ, and through the power of the Holy Spirit.

The Joshua Protocol for Gambling Addiction

Step 1: It's not me, it's just my harmful habit of gambling.

Step 2: God, thank you for your forgiveness, in case I have made any mistakes in how I have dealt with (or failed to address) the issue of gambling.

Step 3: God, thank you for your fellowship; I am not alone in this fight against gambling addiction. Your Holy Spirit indwells me and strengthens me. I need have no fear in this area. Fear is not of God.

Step 4: God, thank you for your perfect discipline. Godly discipline is without punishment, blame, or shame; it is a blessing whereby God teaches, coaches, and encourages me as I prayerfully overcome any gambling addiction, in the name of Jesus Christ and through the power of the Holy Spirit.

The Joshua Protocol for Compulsive, Emotional, or Out-of-Control Spending

Step 1: It's not me, it's just my compulsive money-spending habits.

Step 2: God, thank you for your forgiveness, in case I have made any mistakes in the way I have dealt with (or failed to address) my emotional spending, and the way I manage my money.

Step 3: God, thank you for your fellowship; I am not alone in this fight against compulsive money-spending. Your Holy Spirit indwells me and strengthens me. Please make me more mindful regarding this bad habit. But I need have no fear in this area. Fear is not of God.

Step 4: God, thank you for your perfect discipline. Godly discipline is without punishment, blame, or shame; it is a blessing whereby God teaches, coaches, and encourages me as I prayerfully overcome my compulsive spending habits, in the name of Jesus Christ and through the power of the Holy Spirit.

The Joshua Protocol for Overcoming Pride or Arrogance

Step 1: It's not me, it's just my foolish pride or arrogance.

Step 2: God, thank you for your forgiveness, in case I have made any mistakes in the way I have dealt with (or failed to address) my problem with pride or arrogance.

Step 3: God, thank you for your fellowship; I am not alone in this fight against prideful, egotistical behavior. Your Holy Spirit indwells me and strengthens me. I need have no fear in this area. Fear is not of God.

Step 4: God, thank you for your perfect discipline. Godly discipline is without punishment, blame, or shame; it is a blessing whereby God teaches, coaches, and encourages me as I prayerfully overcome any pride or arrogance, in the name of Jesus Christ and through the power of the Holy Spirit.

The Joshua Protocol for Overcoming Hurtful Sarcasm

Step 1: It's not me, it's just my use of foolish sarcasm.

Step 2: God, thank you for your forgiveness, in case I have made any mistakes in the way I have dealt with (or failed to address) my sarcastic ways.

Step 3: God, thank you for your fellowship; I am not alone in this fight against sarcastic behavior. Your Holy Spirit indwells me and strengthens me. I need have no fear in this area. Fear is not of God.

Step 4: God, thank you for your perfect discipline. Godly discipline is without punishment, blame, or shame; it is a blessing whereby God teaches, coaches, and encourages me as I prayerfully overcome any sarcastic tendencies, in the name of Jesus Christ and through the power of the Holy Spirit.

The Joshua Protocol for Overcoming Jealousy or Envy

Step 1: It's not me, it's just my uncontrolled jealousy or envy.

Step 2: God, thank you for your forgiveness, in case I have made any mistakes in the way I have dealt with (or failed to address) jealousy or envy.

Step 3: God, thank you for your fellowship; I am not alone in this fight against jealous or envious behavior. Your Holy Spirit indwells me and strengthens me. I need have no fear in this area. Fear is not of God.

Step 4: God, thank you for your perfect discipline. Godly discipline is without punishment, blame, or shame; it is a blessing whereby God teaches, coaches, and encourages me as I prayerfully overcome any jealousy or envy, in the name of Jesus Christ and through the power of the Holy Spirit.

The Joshua Protocol for Overcoming Greed

Step 1: It's not me, it's just my uncontrolled greed.

Step 2: God, thank you for your forgiveness, in case I have made any mistakes in the way I have dealt with (or failed to address) my greedy tendencies.

Step 3: God, thank you for your fellowship; I am not alone in this fight against greedy behavior. Your Holy Spirit indwells me and strengthens me. I need have no fear in this area. Fear is not of God.

Step 4: God, thank you for your perfect discipline. Godly discipline is without punishment, blame, or shame; it is a blessing whereby God teaches, coaches, and encourages me as I prayerfully overcome greed, in the name of Jesus Christ and through the power of the Holy Spirit.

The Joshua Protocol for Overcoming Selfishness

Step 1: It's not me, it's just my uncontrolled selfishness.

Step 2: God, thank you for your forgiveness, in case I have made any mistakes in the way I have dealt with (or failed to address) my selfish tendencies.

Step 3: God, thank you for your fellowship; I am not alone in this fight against selfish behavior. Your Holy Spirit indwells me and strengthens me. I need have no fear in this area. Fear is not of God.

Step 4: God, thank you for your perfect discipline. Godly discipline is without punishment, blame, or shame; it is a blessing whereby God teaches, coaches, and encourages me as I prayerfully overcome any selfish tendencies, in the name of Jesus Christ and through the power of the Holy Spirit.

The Joshua Protocol for Overcoming Hoarding Behaviors

Step 1: It's not me, it's just my uncontrolled hoarding behaviors.

Step 2: God, thank you for your forgiveness, in case I have made any mistakes in the way I have dealt with (or failed to address) my problem of hoarding.

Step 3: God, thank you for your fellowship; I am not alone in this fight against hoarding behaviors. Your Holy Spirit indwells me and strengthens me. I need have no fear in this area. Fear is not of God.

Step 4: God, thank you for your perfect discipline. Godly discipline is without punishment, blame, or shame; it is a blessing whereby God teaches, coaches, and encourages me as I prayerfully overcome my problem with hoarding, in the name of Jesus Christ and through the power of the Holy Spirit.

The Joshua Protocol for Overcoming Drug Abuse

Step 1: It's not me, it's just my habit of abusing drugs.

Step 2: God, thank you for your forgiveness, in case I have made any mistakes in how I have dealt with (or failed to address) my drug abuse.

Step 3: God, thank you for your fellowship; I am not alone in this fight against substance abuse. Your Holy Spirit indwells me and strengthens me. I need have no fear in this area. Fear is not of God.

Step 4: God, thank you for your perfect discipline. Godly discipline is without punishment, blame, or shame; it is a blessing whereby God teaches, coaches, and encourages me as I prayerfully overcome my addiction to drugs, in the name of Jesus Christ and through the power of the Holy Spirit.

The Joshua Protocol for Overcoming Alcohol Abuse

Step 1: It's not me, it's just my alcoholism.

Step 2: God, thank you for your forgiveness, in case I have made any mistakes in the way I have dealt with (or failed to address) my alcoholism.

Step 3: God, thank you for your fellowship; I am not alone in this fight against alcoholism. Your Holy Spirit indwells me and strengthens me. I need have no fear in this area. Fear is not of God.

Step 4: God, thank you for your perfect discipline. Godly discipline is without punishment, blame, or shame; it is a blessing whereby God teaches, coaches, and encourages me as I prayerfully overcome my alcoholism, in the name of Jesus Christ and through the power of the Holy Spirit.

The Joshua Protocol to Stop Smoking

Step 1: It's not me, it's just my smoking habit.

Step 2: God, thank you for your forgiveness, in case I have made any mistakes in how I have dealt with (or failed to address) my smoking.

Step 3: God, thank you for your fellowship; I am not alone in this fight to stop smoking. Your Holy Spirit indwells me and strengthens me. I need have no fear in this area. Fear is not of God.

Step 4: God, thank you for your perfect discipline. Godly discipline is without punishment, blame, or shame; it is a blessing whereby God teaches, coaches, and encourages me as I prayerfully overcome my smoking habit, in the name of Jesus Christ and through the power of the Holy Spirit.

The Joshua Protocol for _____

Step 1: It's not me, it's just a bad habit of _____.

Step 2: God, thank you for your forgiveness, in case I have made any mistakes in how I have dealt with (or failed to address) my habit of _____.

Step 3: God, thank you for your fellowship; I am not alone in this fight against _____. Your Holy Spirit indwells me and strengthens me. I need have no fear in this area. Fear is not of God.

Step 4: God, thank you for your perfect discipline. Godly discipline is without punishment, blame, or shame; it is a blessing whereby God teaches, coaches, and encourages me as I prayerfully overcome the habit of _____, in the name of Jesus Christ and through the power of the Holy Spirit.

Appendix 2
Scriptural References

Bible Passages for Better Thought Control

The Counselor emphasized the need for spending time, on a frequent and consistent basis, in prayer and meditation to the Lord. The Joshua Protocol is a useful tool for advancing spiritual transformation and for fending-off unexpected and sudden spiritual attacks. But beyond learning any single technique, the larger message of this book is to encourage readers to develop a broad and rich personal relationship with God. This requires investing time and effort to get to know the Lord through the sacred texts of the Bible. Be sure to avail yourself of the many commentaries, Greek and Hebrew dictionaries, online search engines, and other widely available resources that can help you better understand what the Bible means.

The following are more than one hundred of my favorite biblical Scriptures. I have slowly gathered, pondered, and savored these precious passages for over a decade. Moreover, I believe these short biblical excerpts hold soothing and encouraging messages for people in recovery. I hope readers will take the time and make an effort to glean the wisdom and meanings that may be found in them. For me, these sacred words have been a life-enhancing blessing. I hope they will bless you as well.

Unless otherwise indicated, Scriptural quotations in this appendix are taken from the New American Standard Bible®, Copyright © 1960, 1962, 1963, 1968, 1971, 1972, 1973, 1975, 1977, 1995 by The Lockman Foundation. Used by permission. (www.Lockman.org)

PROVERBS 28:13

He who conceals his transgressions will not prosper, but he who confesses and forsakes them will find compassion.

JOHN 3:20

For everyone who does evil hates the Light, and does not come to the Light for fear that his deeds will be exposed.

PSALMS 101:3 (NIV)

I will set no worthless thing before my eyes; I hate the work of those who fall away; it shall not fasten its grip on me.

JOHN 10:10

The thief comes only to steal and kill and destroy; I came that they may have life, and have it abundantly.

2 TIMOTHY 4:18 (NIV)

The Lord will rescue me from every evil attack and will bring me safely to his heavenly kingdom. To him be glory for ever and ever. Amen.

ROMANS 8:13

For if you are living according to the flesh, you must die; but if by the Spirit you are putting to death the deeds of the body, you will live.

ROMANS 12:2

And do not be conformed to this world, but be transformed by the renewing of your mind, so that you may prove what the will of God is, that which is good and acceptable and perfect.

ROMANS 12:21

Do not be overcome by evil, but overcome evil with good.

GALATIANS 5:24

Now those who belong to Christ Jesus have crucified the flesh with its passions and desires.

EPHESIANS 4:22-24 (NIV)

You were taught, with regard to your former way of life, to put off your old self, which is being corrupted by its deceitful desires; to be made new in the attitude of your minds; and to put on the new self, created to be like God in true righteousness and holiness.

PHILIPPIANS 4:8

Finally, brethren, whatever is true, whatever is honorable, whatever is right, whatever is pure, whatever is lovely, whatever is of good repute, if there is any excellence and if anything worthy of praise, dwell on these things.

LUKE 6:45

The good man out of the good treasure of his heart brings forth what is good; and the evil man out of the evil treasure brings forth what is evil; for his mouth speaks from that which fills his heart.

2 CORINTHIANS 10:3-5

For though we walk in the flesh, we do not war according to the flesh, for the weapons of our warfare are not of the flesh, but divinely powerful for the destruction of fortresses. We are destroying speculations and every lofty thing raised up against the knowledge of God, and we are taking every thought captive to the obedience of Christ.

PHILIPPIANS 4:6-7

Be anxious for nothing, but in everything by prayer and supplication with thanksgiving let your requests be made known to God. And the peace of God, which surpasses all comprehension, will guard your hearts and your minds in Christ Jesus.

ROMANS 8:5-7

For those who are according to the flesh set their minds on the things of the flesh, but those who are according to the Spirit, the things of the Spirit. For the mind set on the flesh is death, but the mind set on the Spirit is life and peace, because the mind set on the flesh is hostile toward God; for it does not subject itself to the law of God, for it is not even able to do so.

PROVERBS 4:25

Let your eyes look directly ahead, and let your gaze be fixed straight in front of you.

2 CORINTHIANS 4:4

The god of this world has blinded the minds of the unbelieving so that they might not see the light of the gospel of the glory of Christ, who is the image of God.

1 PETER 1:13

Therefore, prepare your minds for action, keep sober in spirit, fix your hope completely on the grace to be brought to you at the revelation of Jesus Christ.

JOB 31:1

I have made a covenant with my eyes; how then could I gaze at a virgin?

MARK 7:20-22

And He was saying, "That which proceeds out of the man, that is what defiles the man. For from within, out of the heart of men, proceed the evil thoughts, fornications, thefts, murders, adulteries, deeds of coveting and wickedness, as well as deceit, sensuality, envy, slander, pride and foolishness."

COLOSSIANS 3:2

Set your mind on the things above, not on the things that are on earth.

2 CORINTHIANS 2:16

To the one an aroma from death to death, to the other an aroma from life to life. And who is adequate for these things?

PSALMS 51:10

Create in me a pure heart, O God, and renew a steadfast spirit within me.

1 JOHN 4:4

You are from God, little children, and have overcome them; because greater is He who is in you than he who is in the world.

MATTHEW 7:6

Do not give what is holy to dogs, and do not throw your pearls before swine, lest they trample them under their feet, and turn and tear you to pieces.

DEUTERONOMY 30:11

For this commandment which I command you today is not too difficult for you, nor is it out of reach.

2 CORINTHIANS 7:1 (NIV)

Therefore, since we have these promises, dear friends, let us purify ourselves from everything that contaminates body and spirit, perfecting holiness out of reverence for God.

PSALMS 25:7 (ESV)

Remember not the sins of my youth or my transgressions; according to your steadfast love remember me, for the sake of your goodness, O LORD!

MATTHEW 7:24

Therefore, everyone who hears these words of Mine and acts on them, may be compared to a wise man who built his house on the rock.

GALATIANS 5:16

But I say, walk by the Spirit, and you will not carry out the desire of the flesh.

JOHN 14:15

If you love Me, you will keep My commandments.

MATTHEW 5:8

Blessed are the pure in heart, for they shall see God.

PSALMS 143:10

Teach me to do Your will, For You are my God; Let Your good Spirit lead me on level ground.

ROMANS 8:37 (ESV)

No, in all these things we are more than conquerors through him who loved us.

JAMES 4:7

Submit therefore to God. Resist the devil and he will flee from you.

ISAIAH 61:1

The Spirit of the Lord GOD is upon me, Because the LORD has anointed me to bring good news to the afflicted; he has sent me to bind up the brokenhearted, to proclaim liberty to captives and freedom to prisoners;

ISAIAH 61:7-8

Instead of your shame you will have a double portion, and instead of humiliation they will shout for joy over their portion. Therefore, they will possess a double portion in their land, everlasting joy will be theirs. For I, the LORD, love justice, I hate robbery in the burnt offering; and I will faithfully give them their recompense and make an everlasting covenant with them.

2 CHRONICLES 7:14

And My people who are called by My name humble themselves and pray and seek My face and turn from their wicked ways, then I will hear from heaven, will forgive their sin and will heal their land.

ROMANS 6:16 (AMPLIFIED BIBLE)

Do you not know that when you *continually* offer yourselves to someone to do his will, you are the slaves of the one whom you obey, either [slaves] of sin, which leads to death, or of obedience, which leads to righteousness (right standing with God)?

COLOSSIANS 3:5 (ESV)

Put to death therefore what is earthly in you: sexual immorality, impurity, passion, evil desire, and covetousness, which is idolatry.

1 JOHN 5:21

Little children, guard yourselves from idols.

1 JOHN 2:15

Do not love the world nor the things in the world. If anyone loves the world, the love of the Father is not in him.

Bible Passages for Overcoming Negativity and Pessimism

> Unless otherwise indicated, Scriptural quotations in this appendix are taken from the New American Standard Bible®, Copyright © 1960, 1962, 1963, 1968, 1971, 1972, 1973, 1975, 1977, 1995 by The Lockman Foundation. Used by permission. (www.Lockman.org)

JOHN 3:16

For God so loved the world, that He gave His only begotten Son, that whoever believes in Him shall not perish, but have eternal life.

2 CORINTHIANS 3:18

But we all, with unveiled face, beholding as in a mirror the glory of the Lord, are being transformed into the same image from glory to glory, just as from the Lord, the Spirit.

MATTHEW 11:28

Jesus said, "Come to Me, all who are weary and heavy-laden, and I will give you rest.

PHILIPPIANS 4:6 (TLB)

Don't worry about anything; instead, pray about everything; tell God about your needs and don't forget to thank him for His answers.

PSALMS 120:1 (NIV)

I call on the LORD in my distress, and he answers me.

PSALMS 118:25 (NIV)

LORD, save us! LORD, grant us success!

PHILIPPIANS 3:10-14 (ISV)

I want to know the Messiah. It's not that I have already reached this goal or have already become perfect. But I keep pursuing it, hoping somehow to embrace it just as I have been embraced by the Messiah Jesus. Brothers, I do not consider myself to have embraced it yet. But this one thing I do: Forgetting what lies behind and straining forward to what lies ahead, I keep pursuing the goal to win the prize of God's heavenly call in the Messiah Jesus.

JOHN 10:10

The thief comes only to steal and kill and destroy; I came that they may have life, and have it abundantly.

PHILIPPIANS 4:8

Finally, brethren, whatever is true, whatever is honorable, whatever is right, whatever is pure, whatever is lovely, whatever is of good repute, if there is any excellence and if anything worthy of praise, dwell on these things.

COLOSSIANS 3:15

Let the peace of Christ rule in your hearts and be thankful.

PROVERBS 3:5-6 (NKJV)

Trust in the LORD with all your heart, and lean not on your own understanding; In all your ways acknowledge Him, And He shall direct your paths.

PHILIPPIANS 4:13

I can do all things through Him [Jesus] who strengthens me. *(Brackets added for clarity)*

MARK 10:27; LUKE 18:27; MATTHEW 19:26 (summarized)

All things are possible for God.

EPHESIANS 1:3 (NIV)

Praise be to the God and Father of our Lord Jesus Christ, who has blessed us in the heavenly realms with every spiritual blessing in Christ.

HEBREWS 4:3 (TLB)

For only we who believe God can enter into His place of rest.

1 THESSALONIANS 5:16-18

Rejoice always; pray without ceasing; in everything give thanks; for this is God's will for you in Christ Jesus.

JOHN 16:33 (NIV)

Jesus said, "I have told you these things, so that in me you may have peace. In this world you will have trouble. But take heart! I have overcome the world."

DEUTERONOMY 28:12-13

And the LORD will open for you His good storehouse, the heavens, to give rain to your land in its season and to bless all the work of your hand; and you shall lend to many nations, but you shall not borrow. And the LORD shall make you the head and not the tail, and you shall be above and not beneath.

PHILIPPIANS 4:7

And the peace of God, which surpasses all comprehension, will guard your hearts and your minds in Christ Jesus.

ROMANS 8:16-17

The Spirit Himself testifies with our spirit that we are children of God, and if children, heirs also, heirs of God and fellow heirs with Christ, if indeed we suffer with Him so that we may also be glorified with Him.

ROMANS 8:28 (NIV)

And we know that in all things God works for the good of those who love Him, to those who are called according to His purpose.

ROMANS 8:31-32

What then shall we say to these things? If God *is* for us, who *is* against us? He who did not spare His own Son, but delivered Him over for us all, how will He not also with Him freely give us all things?

JAMES 1:2-4 (TLB)

Dear brothers, is your life full of difficulties and temptations? Then be happy, for when the way is rough, your patience has a chance to grow. So let it grow and do not try to squirm out of your problems. When your patience is finally in full bloom, then you will be ready for anything, strong in character, full and complete.

1 PETER 5:9 (TLB)

Stand firm when he [Satan] attacks. Trust the Lord; and remember that other Christians all around the world are going through these same sufferings too. *(Brackets added for clarity)*

ISAIAH 40:29-31

He gives strength to the weary, and to him who lacks might He increases power. Those who wait for the LORD will gain new strength; they will mount up with wings like eagles, they will run and not get tired, they will walk and not become weary.

1 CORINTHIANS 10:13 (ESV)

No temptation has overtaken you that is not common to man. God is faithful, and he will not let you be tempted beyond your ability, but with the temptation he will also provide the way of escape, that you may be able to endure it.

MATTHEW 8:13

And Jesus said to the centurion, "Go; it shall be done for you as you have believed." And the servant was healed that *very* moment.

1 THESSALONIANS 5:18

In [during] everything give thanks; for this is the will of God. *(Brackets added for clarity)*

GALATIANS 6:9 (ESV)

And let us not grow weary of doing good, for in due season we will reap, if we do not give up.

PSALMS 37:34 (TLB)

Don't be impatient for the Lord to act! Keep traveling steadily along His pathway and in due season He will honor you with every blessing.

HEBREWS 4:16 (AMP)

Let us then fearlessly and confidently and boldly draw near to the throne of grace—the throne of God's unmerited favor.

PSALMS 91:11-12

For He will give His angels charge concerning you, to guard you in all your ways. They will bear you up in their hands, that you do not strike your foot against a stone.

PSALMS 37:7

Rest in the LORD and wait patiently for Him.

JOHN 16:23-24 (TLB)

Jesus said: "You can go directly to the Father and ask Him, and He will give you what you ask for because you use my name. Ask, using my name, and you will receive, and your cup of joy will overflow."

PSALMS 51:10 *(The Message)*

God, make a fresh start in me, shape a Genesis week from the chaos of my life.

ZECHARIAH 4:6 (NIV)

So he said to me, "This is the word of the LORD to Zerubbabel: 'Not by might nor by power, but by my Spirit,' says the LORD Almighty."

ISAIAH 54:17 (AMP)

But no weapon that is formed against you shall prosper, and every tongue that shall rise against you in judgment you shall show to be in the wrong. This [peace, righteousness, security, triumph over opposition] is the heritage of the servants of the Lord.

PSALMS 34:19

Many are the afflictions of the righteous; but the Lord delivers him out of them all.

PSALMS 46:10 (ESV)

Be still and know that I am God.

PHILIPPIANS 1:28 (AMP)

And do not [for a moment] be frightened or intimidated in anything by your opponents and adversaries, for such [constancy and fearlessness] will be a clear sign (proof and seal) to them of [their impending] destruction; but [a sure token and evidence] of your deliverance and salvation, and that from God.

ZECHARIAH 12:10 (AMP)

God said "And I will pour out upon the house of David and upon the inhabitants of Jerusalem the Spirit of grace or unmerited favor, and supplication."

MATTHEW 6:25-27 (NIV)

Therefore, I tell you, do not worry about your life, what you will eat or drink. Look at the birds of the air; they do not sow or reap or store away in barns, and yet your heavenly Father feeds them. Are you not much more valuable than they? Who of you by worrying can add a single hour to his life?

COLOSSIANS 3:2 (AMP)

Set your minds and keep them set on what is above—the higher things—not on the things that are on the earth.

HEBREWS 11:8 (NIV)

By faith Abraham, when called to go to a place he would later receive as his inheritance, obeyed and went, even though he did not know where he was going.

2 CORINTHIANS 5:7 (NIV)

We live by faith, not by sight.

ISAIAH 41:10-14 (NIV)

So do not fear, for I am with you; do not be dismayed, for I am your God. I will strengthen you and help you; I will uphold you with my righteous right hand. All who rage against you will surely be ashamed and disgraced; those who oppose you will be as nothing and perish. Though you search for your enemies, you will not find them. Those who wage war against you will be as nothing at all. For I am the Lord, your God, who takes hold of your right hand and says to you, Do not fear; I will help you. Do not be afraid, O worm Jacob, O Israel.

ROMANS 8:24 (ESV)

For in this hope we were saved. Now hope that is seen is not hope. For who hopes for what he sees?

ROMANS 12:17 (NIV)

Do not repay anyone evil for evil.

2 CHRONICLES 20:2-3 (AMP)

It was told Jehoshaphat, a great multitude has come against you from beyond the [Dead] Sea.... Then Jehoshaphat feared, and set himself [determinedly, as his vital need] to seek the Lord.

MARK 9:24 (NIV)

Immediately the [demon possessed] boy's father exclaimed [while crying tears before Jesus], "I do believe; help me overcome my unbelief!" [my weak faith] *(Brackets added for clarity)*

HEBREWS 10:23 (NIV)

Let us hold unswervingly to the hope we profess, for he who promised is faithful.

ISAIAH 55:9 (NIV)

As the heavens are higher than the earth, so are my ways higher than your ways and my thoughts than your thoughts.

MARK 11:24-25 (TLB)

Jesus said "Listen to me! You can pray for *anything*, and *if you believe, you have it*; it's yours! But when you are praying, first forgive anyone you are holding a grudge against, so that your Father in heaven will forgive you your sins too."

JEREMIAH 9:7 (TLB)

Therefore, the Lord of Hosts says "I will melt them in a crucible of affliction. I will refine them [to remove the dross] and test them like metal. What else can I do with them?" *(Brackets added for clarity)*

MATTHEW 6:34 (TLB)

Jesus said "So don't be anxious about tomorrow. God will take care of your tomorrow too. Live one day at a time."

ROMANS 15:13

Now may the God of hope fill you with all joy and peace in believing, so that you will abound in hope by the power of the Holy Spirit.

NEHEMIAH 8:10 (ISV)

The joy of the Lord is your strength.

DEUTERONOMY 31:6 (NIV)

Be strong and courageous. Do not be afraid or terrified because of them, for the Lord your God goes with you; he will never leave you nor forsake you.

2 KINGS 6:17 (NIV)

And Elisha prayed, "Open his eyes, LORD, so that he may see." Then the LORD opened the servant's eyes, and he looked and saw the hills full of horses and chariots of fire all around Elisha.

PSALMS 55:22 (NIV)

Cast your cares on the Lord and he will sustain you; he will never let the righteous be shaken.

PSALMS 19:14

May these words of my mouth and this meditation of my heart be pleasing in your sight, Lord, my Rock and my Redeemer.

EPHESIANS 4:29-30 (NIV)

Do not let any unwholesome talk come out of your mouths, but only what is helpful for building others up according to their needs, that it may benefit those who listen.

LUKE 19:10 (ESV)

For the Son of Man came to seek and to save the lost.

MATTHEW 7:7

Ask, and it will be given to you; seek, and you will find; knock, and it will be opened to you.

HEBREWS 13:8

Jesus Christ is the same yesterday and today and forever.

1 PETER 5:6-7 (NKJV)

Therefore, humble yourselves under the mighty hand of God, that He may exalt you in due time, casting all your care upon Him, for He cares for you.

1 SAMUEL 3:9

And Eli said to Samuel, "Go lie down, and it shall be if He calls you, that you shall say, 'Speak, LORD, for Your servant is listening.'"

HEBREWS 11:1 (NIV)

Now faith is confidence in what we hope for and assurance about what we do not see.

JOHN 11:40

Jesus said to her, "Did I not say to you that if you believe, you will see the glory of God?"

JOHN 14:1

Jesus said, "Do not let your heart be troubled; believe in God, believe also in Me.

JOHN 14:6

Jesus said to him, "I am the way, and the truth, and the life; no one comes to the Father but through Me."

2 CORINTHIANS 3:17

Now the Lord is the Spirit, and where the Spirit of the Lord is, there is liberty.

PSALM 34:8

O taste and see that the LORD is good; How blessed is the man who takes refuge in Him!

Endnotes

Endnotes for the Introduction

1. When I was about to finish work on this book, I returned to the Counselor to ask him for a few more details about his education and background. He was wary about telling me too much, for fear that his identity would later be discovered. But he finally shared that his undergraduate studies in psychology took place at the California State University, at Chico. Moreover, he has three master's degrees, including one in education and another in divinity from an unnamed university in South Florida. Additionally, he holds two doctorates: one in marriage and family counseling, and a second in theology. Both of his terminal degrees are from an unnamed school on the West Coast of the United States. Much about the Counselor remains a mystery; the man will forever be a mystical enigma.
2. Matthew 26:41 and Mark 14:38 (NIV)
3. (Lewis, *The Screwtape Letters*, chapter 8)

Endnotes for Counseling Session 1

4. Dr. Tanzi, in *Super Brain*, talks about how the "neuro" part of neuroplasticity comes from the word *neuron*. A neuron is a nerve cell that transmits electrical impulses. Every human being has a brain that contains many billions of neurons. These neurons act like circuitry within the brain, and are important building blocks in the formation of the brain. Dr. Tanzi further explains that "plasticity" refers to any object that is malleable or can be reshaped or reformed. So, the term

neuroplasticity suggests that neurons are not fixed or "hard wired" in place. Instead, the circuitry of the human brain can be remodeled, "rewired," and improved. The brain, itself, can be "remapped" or have its electrical circuitry rerouted along different pathways. In this way, with much hard work and consistent effort it is possible to reformat or retrain the human brain to function and think differently. This offers the potential for us to transform our bad habits and negative thought processes into healthier and more positive ones. See *Super Brain*, p. 22.

5 Norman Doidge says that the term neuroplasticity became widely known in the year 2007. See *The Brain's Way of Healing*, page 240.
6 For additional references on the subject of neuroplasticity, consult the Bibliography at the end of this book.
7 (Doidge, *The Brain's Way of Healing*, page XV)
8 (Tanzi, 2012, p. 167)
9 I want to address a controversy that manifested itself during the field testing of the manuscript for this book. The issue had to do with whether the apostle Paul used the "historical present" tense when writing his letter to the Romans. Such a theological debate is not a focus of this work. I mention it here, only because I do not want to distract my readers from the main themes presented in this text. For my purposes, I prefer not to engage in any controversy dealing with whether Paul wrote Romans 7 using an historical "flash back" literary technique. Many Internet blogs exist whereby interested readers may engage in lively debates over Paul's salvation, and about how the specific timing of events in Paul's life may have impacted his New Testament writings.
10 Romans 7:15 and 20, ESV
11 Genesis 1:26
12 Galatians 2:20, NIV
13 1 Corinthians 12:27, NIV
14 2 Corinthians 5:20
15 Romans 8:17
16 Romans 6:11
17 Galatians 2:20
18 *The Exorcist*, feature film, 1973.
19 Matthew 11:12 (ESV) Jesus said, "From the days of John the Baptist until now the kingdom of heaven has suffered violence [*biázō*], and the violent [*biastēs*] take it by force [*harpázō*]." (Brackets, underlines, and Greek translations added) Adapted from Thayer's Greek Lexicon,

translations: *biázō*, βιάζω, to force, as in "the kingdom of heaven is taken by violence, carried by storm, i.e. a share in the heavenly kingdom is sought for with the most ardent zeal and the intensest exertion;" *biastēs*, βιάζω, violent men, who strive to obtain the *privileges* of the Kingdom of Heaven with utmost eagerness and effort. *harpázō*, ἁρπάζω, to take, or "to snatch out or away." SOURCE: *Blue Letter Bible (http://www.blueletterbible.org)* Definition of privilege, noun. A grant to an individual, corporation, etc., of a special right or immunity, under certain conditions. SOURCE: *www.dictionary.reference.com*

20 James 1:2
21 Philippians 4:7

Endnotes for Counseling Session 2

22 Joshua 9:14
23 Isaiah 61:3
24 John 3:16, NIV
25 John 14:16
26 See 1 John 4:18 in the Greek translation, *kolasis (pronounced:* ko'-lä-sēs), meaning "correction, punishment, penalty."
27 Romans 12:21

Endnotes for Counseling Session 3

28 (Schwartz and Gladding, You Are Not Your Brain 2012, 148)
29 Be sure to also visit Dr. Schwartz's website at www.jeffreymschwartz.com
30 Visit http://feelinggood.com/
31 Matthew 10:19-20, NIV. From the Greek, πατήρ patḗr, pat-ayr'; a "father"—father, parent.
32 Mark 13:11, NIV. *Hágios pneûma*, from the Greek, ἅγιος *hágios*, hag'-ee-os; sacred—(most) holy (one, thing), saint. And from πνεῦμα *pneûma*, pnyoo'-mah; a spirit, i.e. (human) the rational soul, (by implication) vital principle, mental disposition, etc., or (superhuman) an angel, demon, or (divine) God, Christ's spirit, the Holy Spirit.
33 1 Corinthians 10:13, NIV
34 1 Corinthians 3:16, Romans 8:9, et al.
35 1 Corinthians 15:49, Philippians 3:21
36 Revelation 21:1

37 Galatians 5:1, NIV
38 Throughout this book, I make frequent references to "the cross." Crucifixion was an ancient method of capital punishment that was infamously used by the government of the Roman Empire. In antiquity, Rome used this savage and cruel method of discipline to torture and execute criminals and political enemies of the state. Additionally, the process of crucifixion offered the added benefit of instilling terror amongst conquered populations. This fear allowed Rome to maintain its political domination over diverse people groups throughout a vast territory that was, at one time, controlled by the Roman Emperor.
39 John 19:30
40 (Leaf, 2013, p.64)
41 Ephesians 5:26
42 1 John 4:8, NIV
43 1 John 4:18, NIV
44 1 John 1:9, TLB
45 Romans 8:1, ESV
46 Philippians 4:7
47 1 Corinthians 13:12
48 Romans 12:21

Endnotes for Counseling Session 4

49 Ask most kidney dialysis patients, and they will tell you their dialysis treatments are very taxing upon their bodies. Yet, the benefits outweigh the discomforts. There is a life-giving cleansing of the dialysis patient's blood from deadly toxins that build-up and threaten to kill the person. The dialysis process is somewhat similar to when God cleanses us of our toxic, poisonous, or otherwise sinful actions. The medical metaphor is both compelling and useful.
50 (Collins, 2010, p. 134)
51 The actual quote from author Henry James was "Excellence does not require perfection."
52 Revelation 12:10
53 2 Corinthians 5:17
54 C.S. Lewis discusses God's mastery over time in *Mere Christianity* (see book 4, chapter 3: "Time and Beyond Time").
55 Revelation 20:10

56 John 3:16
57 Revelation 12:7-9
58 Romans 8:15, Romans 8:23, Ephesians 1:5
59 (Tanzi, 2012, p. 136)
60 1 Corinthians 15:31
61 Luke 23:34
62 Deuteronomy 30:11
63 Matthew 19:16–23, Mark 10:17–23, and Luke 18:18–24
64 1 Corinthians 9:27
65 God wants us to know Him and to be His friend. See Hosea 6:6, Exodus 33:11-17, 2 Chronicles 20:7, Job 29:4, Isaiah 41:8, Acts 13:22, James 2:23
66 1 Thessalonians 5:17 (ESV)
67 I believe the Counselor obtained his "mirror" references from 2 Corinthians 3:18
68 Psalm 34:8
69 (Doidge, *The Brain That Changes Itself*, p. 105)
70 Romans 12:2
71 See John 3:28-29, Mark 2:19-20, Revelation 19:7-9, Revelation 21:9, 2 Corinthians 11:2
72 See Exodus 20:3-6, Colossians 3:5, 1 John 5:21, 1 Corinthians 10:14
73 Genesis 3:18
74 Matthew 18:4
75 (Lewis, *The Screwtape Letters*, chapter 18)
76 See Matthew 5:48 (NIV)
77 (Lewis, *Mere Christianity*, chapter 9)
78 See Isaiah 64:4, 1 Corinthians 2:9, and 2 Corinthians 12:1-7
79 Matthew 19:12
80 1 Corinthians 7:7-9
81 Isaiah 26:3 (NIV)
82 I do not want to confuse readers by bringing in too many foreign language translations, but the Greek word used in the New Testament for peace is εἰρήνη, *eirēnē*, and is pronounced: ā-rā'-nā or i-ray'-nay. The Greek translation of the word *peace* includes the ideas of achieving a sense of security, safety, prosperity, felicity, or of a tranquil state of a soul assured of its salvation through Christ, and so fearing nothing from God and content with its earthly lot, of whatsoever sort that is.
83 Colossians 3:15 (NIV)
84 Philippians 4:7 (NIV)
85 John 16:33 (NIV)

Endnotes for Counseling Session 5

86 (Wright, 2011, p. 205)
87 Exodus 34:6, Psalms 103:8
88 Ephesians 4:26-27, James 1:19-20, Psalms 37:8-9, Proverbs 15:18, Proverbs 16:32, Proverbs 19:11, Ecclesiastes 7:9
89 Galatians 5:6
90 Deuteronomy 32:35
91 John 2:3-11
92 (Carlson, 2011, pp. 44, 79, 97, 99, and 124)
93 Matthew 19:26
94 Hebrews 4:16, Amplified Bible, Classic Edition
95 Daniel 3:27
96 Luke 23:34
97 John 21:21-22
98 Isaiah 55:9
99 In an early draft of this book, one highly-esteemed reviewer shared his concerns about this section, saying it was "A little bit dangerous to assume that God has found a way to save someone who has shown absolutely no fruit" of repentance or transformation. The reviewer suggested that we cannot really take any stance or make assumptions regarding the state of such a person's salvation.

   In response to the esteemed reviewer, I think the Counselor would say it is even more "dangerous" to imply that God is somehow limited in His ability to bestow favor, and to grant clemency and the gift of salvation to His children. All things are possible for God (Mark 10:27; Luke 18:27; and Matthew 19:26). Moreover, love appears to hold the key. God seems willing to break some of His own rules when motivated to do so by love. (1 Peter 4:8) We should probably have faith that God can find a way to connect with those people who seem the most distant from Him.
100 Galatians 5:24
101 1 Corinthians 15:31
102 Ephesians 4:23

Endnotes for Counseling Session 6

103 (Amnesty and Pardon - Clemency Powers In The Twentieth Century 2002-2015)
104 Isaiah 26:3
105 Literally in the Greek, μεταμορφόω metamorphóō, met-am-or-fo'-o, or to transform or transfigure.
106 (Helmstetter, The Power of Neuroplasticity 2013, 113-123)
107 Matthew 5:44; Luke 6:28, NIV
108 (Doidge, *The Brain's Way of Healing*, p. 13)
109 1 Thessalonians 5:16
110 2 Corinthians 5:17
111 Daniel 10:13-14, *The Message*
112 John 10:10

Endnotes for the Conclusion

113 1 Corinthians 15:35-49
114 I later learned that "emergence" is most commonly a scientific term used in physics to explain how complex physical structures are created within nature. My research showed that the term may also be applied to religion, the arts, and the humanities, but these discussions lie outside the scope of this book.
115 See Psalm 9:16 and Genesis 50:20

Bibliography

n.d. *Advanced Nervous System Physiology: Neuroplasticity.* Matt Jensen. Accessed July 17, 2015. https://www.khanacademy.org/science/health-and-medicine/nervous-system-and-sensory-infor/neural-cells-and-neurotransmitters/v/neuroplasticity.

2002-2015. *Amnesty and Pardon - Clemency Powers In The Twentieth Century.* Accessed July 5, 2015. http://law.jrank.org/pages/507/Amnesty-Pardon-Clemency-powers-in-twentieth-century.html#ixzz3eTEoAMIn.

1993. *Shadowlands.* Directed by Richard Attenborough. Performed by Debra Winger Anthony Hopkins.

Barnes, Albert. 1870. *Albert Barnes' Commentary on the New Testament.* Accessed February 28, 2015. http://www.studylight.org/commentaries/bnb/view.cgi?bk=43&ch=20.

Bevere, John. 2003. *The Bait of Satan: Your Response Determines Your Future.* Palmer Lake, Colorado: Messenger Media, a division of John Bevere Ministries.

Blue Letter Bible. 2016. May. www.blueletterbible.org.

Burns, David D. n.d. Accessed October 2014. http://feelinggood.com/.

—. 1989. *The Feeling Good Handbook: Using the New Mood Therapy in Everyday Life.* New York: William Morrow and Company, Inc.

Carlson, Dwight L. 2000. *Overcoming Hurts & Anger: Finding Freedom from Negative Emotions.* Eugene, Oregon: Harvest House Publishers.

Carnes, Patrick. 2001. *Out of the Shadows (Understanding Sexual Addiction).* Center City, Minnesota: Hazelden.

Collins, George N. 2010. *Breaking the Cycle: Free Yourself from Sex Addiction, Porn Obsession, and Shame.* Oakland: New Harbinger Publications, Inc.

Counselor, The, interview by Eric Roderiques. 2013-2014. *Licensed Marriage and Family Therapist* (October-February).

Doidge, Norman. n.d. Accessed July 18, 2015. http://www.normandoidge.com/.

—. 2007. *The Brain That Changes Itself: Stories of Personal Triumph from the Frontiers of Brain Science.* New York: Viking.

—. 2015. *The Brain's Way of Healing: Remarkable Discoveries and Recoveries from the Frontiers of Neuroplasticity.* New York: Viking.

Helmstetter, Shad. n.d. *Internet Web Site.* Accessed July 18, 2015. http://shadhelmstetter.com/.

—. 2013. *The Power of Neuroplasticity.* Gulf Breeze, Florida: Park Avenue Press.

Jantz, Gregory L. 2009. *Controlling Your Anger Before it Controls You.* Grand Rapids: Revell Books.

Jill L. Kays, Psy.D., Robin A. Hurley, M.D., Katherine H. Taber, Ph.D. 2012. "The Dynamic Brain: Neuroplasticity and Mental Health." *The Journal of Neuropsychiatry and Clinical Neurosciences* 118-124. Accessed July 17, 2015. http://neuro.psychiatryonline.org/doi/full/10.1176/appi.neuropsych.12050109.

Leaf, Caroline. 2013. *Switch On Your Brain.* Grand Rapids, Michigan: Baker Publishing Group.

Leman, Kevin. 2003. *Sheet Music: Uncovering the Secrets of Sexual Intimacy in Marriage.* Illinois: Tyndale House Publishers, Inc.

Lewis, Clive Staples. 1952. *Mere Christianity.* New York: HarperCollins.

—. 1946. *The Great Divorce.* New York: HarperCollins.

—. 1940. *The Problem of Pain.* New York: HarperCollins.

—. 1942. *The Screwtape Letters.* New York: HarperCollins.

Meyer, Joyce. 2002. *Battlefield of the Mind.* New York: Warner.

Mintle, Linda. 2002. *Breaking Free from Anger & Unforgiveness.* Lake Mary: Siloam.

Morgan Scott Peck, M.D. 2005. *Glimpses of the Devil.* New York: Free Press, Simon & Schuster.

—. 1998. *People of the Lie.* New York: Touchstone, Simon & Schuster.

Roberts, Ted. 2010. *Seven Pillars of Freedom (Pure Desire Men's Workbook).* Gresham, Oregon: Pure Desire Ministries International.

Schwartz, Jeffrey M. n.d. *You Are Not Your Brain.* Accessed October 2014. http://jeffreymschwartz.com/.

Schwartz, Jeffrey M., and Rebecca Gladding. 2012. *You Are Not Your Brain.* New York: Penguin Group.

Sentis Pty Ltd. 2012. *Neuroplasticity.* Accessed July 11, 2015. https://www.youtube.com/watch?v=ELpfYCZa87g.

Tanzi, Deepak Chopra and Rudolph E. 2012. *Super Brain (Unleashing the Explosive Power of Your Mind to Maximize Health, Happiness, and Spiritual Well-Being).* New York: Harmony Books-Random House.

n.d. "The Refiner's Fire." *Meaning of Shalom.* Accessed September 11, 2017. https://www.therefinersfire.org/meaning_of_shalom.htm.

Welton, Jonathan. 2012. *Eyes of Honor - Training for Purity & Righteousness*. Shippensburg, PA: Destiny Image Publishers, Inc.

Wiles, Jeremy & Tiana. 2013. *Conquer Series: The Battle Plan for Purity (Study Guide)*. West Palm Beach, Florida: Kingdom Works Studios.

Wright, H. Norman. 2011. *A Better Way to Think: How Positive Thoughts Can Change Your Life*. Grand Rapids: Revell Books.

Zaslow, Rabbi David. n.d. "The Deeper Meaning of Shalom." Accessed September 9, 2017. http://rabbidavidzaslow.com/the-deeper-meaning-of-shalom/.

Index

A

a brand new paradigm 120
abuse xxiv, xxx, 11, 88
affective therapy 43
Ainsworth, Mary 90
angels 35, 54, 77, 121, 155
anger xxi, 21, 54, 82, 83, 84, 85,
    88, 90, 93, 95, 97, 104,
    106, 120
Apartheid 106
the apostle Paul 3, 7, 8, 37, 44,
    57, 58, 65, 76, 83, 90, 96,
    100, 107
attachment theory 90

B

bad life history 20
Battlefield of the Mind 57
behavior modification 20, 109
Beta-endorphins 71
betrayal 90
the Bodyguard 34
book of Daniel 116
book of Joshua xxv, 17, 41
Bowlby, John 90
Burns, David D. 34, 171

C

career sex addicts 69
Carlson, Dwight L. 90, 172
celibacy 77
Cognitive Behavioral Therapy
    (CBT) 43
the Counselor xxi, xxii, xxiii,
    xxiv, xxv, xxvii, 1, 2, 4, 8, 9,
    10, 11, 13, 17, 20, 22, 23, 24,
    25, 29, 30, 31, 32, 33, 34, 35,
    36, 37, 38, 39, 40, 41, 43, 44,
    56, 58, 59, 61, 62, 63, 64, 65,
    66, 67, 68, 69, 71, 81, 83, 84,
    85, 86, 87, 88, 90, 91, 94, 96,
    99, 100, 102, 104, 105, 107,
    113, 119, 120, 121, 141
C.S. Lewis xxviii, 44, 52, 101, 112,
    121, 122

D

debaucheries 68
Deepak Chopra 1
devil 17, 19, 23, 25, 26, 48, 49, 51,
    52, 53, 117, 122
discipline 23, 24, 26, 39, 42, 51, 56,
    59, 61, 96, 109, 110, 111

Doidge, Norman 64, 65, 164, 172
Dostoevsky 71

E

emotional wounds 2, 97
erectile dysfunction 64
erotic 61
the eroticism movement 69
The Exorcist 10

F

false ideas about pleasure 69
fantasy xxiv, 38, 59
fear and anxiety 55
Feeling Good 34
fellowship 22, 26, 51, 56, 95, 109, 110, 111
fetishes 66
The Fifteen-Minute Rule 33
fight or flight survival response 5
forgiveness 20, 25, 102

G

Garden of Eden xxviii, 59, 62, 66
Ghost 112
Gibeonites 18, 19, 22, 24, 26, 40, 41, 100, 102
Glimpses of the Devil 10
God xxii, xxvi, xxvii, xxix, 2, 3, 7, 8, 9, 10, 11, 12, 13, 14, 18, 19, 21, 22, 23, 24, 25, 26, 35, 36, 37, 39, 40, 42, 43, 44, 47, 48, 51, 52, 53, 54, 55, 58, 59, 62, 63, 64, 65, 66, 68, 69, 72, 73, 74, 75, 76, 77, 83, 84, 88, 90, 91, 92, 93, 94, 95, 96, 101, 102, 103, 104, 105, 106, 108, 109, 110, 111, 113, 116, 119, 120, 121, 122, 123, 141, 143, 144, 145, 146, 150, 151, 152, 153, 154, 155, 156, 157, 158, 160
God as our husband 66
God becomes our lover 65
good overpowers bad 20
grace 24, 26, 76, 82, 88, 91, 92, 106, 145, 155, 157
grain of sand into a pearl 10, 88, 95, 96
The Great Divorce 112
guilt 7, 39, 48, 51, 64, 66

H

Haiti 10
Harvard Medical School 55
health and wholeness 68
healthy human sexuality 62
Hebrew xxv, 17, 20, 100, 103, 106
heirs with Christ 54
Higher Power 11
hijacked emotions and brain 111
H. Norman Wright 82
horrors of combat 14

I

idolatry 68
idols 69
imago Dei 94
invisible adversaries 122
It's not me 6, 40, 108, 109, 110, 111

J

Jesus xxviii, 3, 9, 17, 20, 21, 23, 25, 37, 40, 41, 42, 43, 44, 47, 56, 57, 66, 72, 76, 77, 84, 88, 90, 94, 100, 102, 104, 113, 119,

123, 145, 151, 152, 153, 155, 156, 159, 160
Joseph and Potiphar's wife 114
Joshua xxiv, xxvii, 17, 18, 19, 20, 22, 23, 24, 34, 37, 39, 47, 48, 49, 51, 55, 56, 58, 61, 81, 90, 93, 100, 102, 108, 109, 111, 113, 115, 116, 117, 122, 141
Joshua Protocol xxiv, xxvii, 19, 20, 22, 23, 24, 34, 37, 39, 47, 48, 49, 51, 55, 56, 58, 61, 81, 90, 93, 100, 102, 108, 109, 111, 113, 115, 116, 117, 122, 141
Joyce Meyer 57, 105

L

Leaf, Caroline 41, 172
learn how to feel again 69
little kids 72
the little red lizard 112
loss of orgasm 69
Lover of God 61
lower brain 4, 6, 9, 31, 37, 42, 93, 108, 109, 113, 116, 120
Lucifer 53, 54

M

medical anger 83
meditation 11, 12, 122, 141
Mere Christianity 44, 101
mind xxv, 1, 5, 11, 13, 20, 21, 23, 24, 29, 31, 32, 34, 36, 38, 40, 43, 44, 47, 51, 62, 64, 66, 67, 68, 71, 81, 85, 88, 91, 93, 95, 96, 106, 107, 108, 109, 120, 143, 144, 145
mirror analogy 62, 63, 65, 100
Morgan Scott Peck 10

morphine 71

N

neuroplasticity 1, 2, 33, 43, 56, 81, 88, 91, 96, 115, 120

O

Obsessive-Compulsive Disorder 33
optimal lifestyle 68
orgies 68
oxytocin 71

P

pain in healing 56
parasympathetic nervous system 86
People of the Lie 10
perfect peace 77
personal relationship with God 49, 59, 66, 68, 92, 122, 141
porn addicts 64
pornography 37, 38, 69, 115
Potiphar's wife 114
prayer 11, 18, 19, 21, 23, 24, 25, 26, 40, 48, 51, 61, 90, 96, 108, 116, 122, 141
primal 4, 6, 7, 31, 42, 87, 91, 93, 107, 108, 109, 121

R

reattribute 33
recovery 49, 115, 116, 122, 141
refocus 33
relabel 33
relapse 116
revalue 33

S

Satan 10, 20, 22, 23, 25, 26, 40, 48, 49, 51, 52, 53, 54, 55, 109, 117, 120, 122, 154
Schwartz, Jeffrey M. xv, 30, 33, 34, 173
Screwtape Letters xxviii, 52, 121
self-actualization 66
self-medicate pain 78
sensory pleasure 64
sensuality 63
sex orgies 58
Sex Perfected 59
sexuality 63
sex will die 69
shalom 77, 103, 104, 106, 107, 118
shame xxx, 7, 25, 39, 48, 51, 64, 66
sin xxx, xxxi, 7, 9, 18, 20, 21, 24, 25, 37, 40, 47, 57, 62, 66, 68, 105, 107, 108, 112, 120, 123
Song of Solomon 59, 62, 75
South Africa 106
South African Truth and Reconciliation Commission 106
spiritual anger 84
spiritual royalty 54
spiritual warfare 22, 26, 117, 122
suffocating fire 121
Super Brain 1
supernatural relationship with God 68
sympathetic nervous system 86
synthetic drugs 66

T

Tanzi, Rudolph "Rudy" 1, 2, 3, 4, 55

thank messages 26, 56, 109, 121
Theology as a "map" 101
transcendental relation 73
transformed 19
transforming xxix, 25, 114, 120, 123
Type-A perfectionists 87

U

upper brain 4, 6, 7, 31, 34, 88, 91, 95, 108

V

vasopressin 71
Vietnam 14

Y

You Are Not Your Brain 30

Take the "process" and overlay it here

CPSIA information can be obtained
at www.ICGtesting.com
Printed in the USA
BVHW091142061220
595043BV00012B/362